T0058430

Tarot:
Novice to Pro
in One Book

Tarot:
Novice to Pro
in One Book

Tarot:
Novice to Pro
in One Book

Colette Brown

Winchester, UK
Washington, USA

First published by Dodona Books, 2011
Dodona Books is an imprint of John Hunt Publishing Ltd., Laurel House, Station Approach,
Alresford, Hants, SO24 9JH, UK
office1@o-books.net
www.o-books.com

For distributor details and how to order please visit the 'Ordering' section on our website.

ISBN: 978 1 84694 965 4

A CIP catalogue record for this book is available from the British Library.

Design: Lee Nash

Printed in the UK by CPI Antony Rowe
Printed in the USA by Offset Paperback Mfrs, Inc

We operate a distinctive and ethical publishing philosophy in all
areas of our business, from our global network of authors to
production and worldwide distribution.

CONTENTS

CONTENTS

To my daughters, Jennifer and Jillian, my reasons for being.
To Jim for all love and support.

Introduction

The Tarot consists of 78 cards. These are split into the 22 cards of the Major Arcana and the 56 cards of the Minor Arcana.

Life is fully reflected in these 78 cards. The range is from major life events such as birth, adolescence and even death, to the challenges of life including love, family, health, spirituality and career. More mundane, everyday aspects such as finances, responsibilities and mood are also represented.

The Major Arcana can be viewed as a rite of passage, starting in childhood and ending with final illumination and revelation. An alternative view of the Major Arcana, popular in times past, regards it as the complete view of life and society where good and evil compete for influence.

Every card can be viewed as having a positive or a negative influence and a card should be read as part of a spread to provide an in-depth picture. I personally do not read reversed cards as negative or the opposite of its traditional meaning as I feel that the deck is perfectly balanced as it is. Instead, I ask the reader to "feel" whether the card is exerting its positive or negative influence on the situation under investigation. These "feelings" only come after plenty of practice and a good understanding of the various combinations of cards found within the spread. It also requires a degree of confidence and self-belief. Obviously, this is easier for some people than others so the length of time required to gain the "feelings" can vary.

It is, of course, preferable to use the complete deck of 78 cards for readings. However, to begin with, time will be spent examining the Major Arcana in depth. The set spreads will be practiced using only these cards. As the book continues, new spreads will start to incorporate the Minor Arcana cards until an understanding of the full Tarot has been gained.

Learn the card meanings and follow up on this by doing the

set homework. If you find it hard to do homework without a real person there, try to imagine the inquirer and give them a personality and a name. If this is too hard, then sit a cuddly toy or photo of someone in front of you and talk to 'them' as you do the homework. There are no straightforward answers. You will need to combine the knowledge of the cards with your own intuition of the situation and see what you feel. That is why there are no answers provided. Each question is based on a real life client encounter which combined both knowledge of the cards plus intuition. The answers you give at the start may be different if you redo them again later, due to your advanced understanding and connection with the tarot. Try the questions a few times and try to add depth to each one. It is really only when you have real life enquirer that it will all gel for you.

The card descriptions are based on the meanings illustrated by standard and traditional decks. Therefore, you will need to study from one of these decks e.g. Rider Waite, Morgan Greer. These traditional decks make a great starting point and once you have mastered them, don't be afraid to let YOUR tarot deck choose YOU! You may be attracted to a deck that more suits your spiritual outlook, culture or aesthetic. Once a deck truly speaks to you intuitively, you will feel completely at home with the tarot.

Once you have completed this book, you should have a good knowledge and understanding of card meanings, different spreads and of ethics and how to set up a professional reading. It will then be up to you to practice, practice, and practice!!! Spend time accruing knowledge slowly and methodically. Don't rush it or you will forget what you have learned. Repeat spreads. Meditate on a card each night. Just look at it and lose yourself in its wonderful imagery. Live the card. Feel it. Don't underestimate the layers of knowledge in each card. What you put in, you will get out. You will never stop learning new things about each card. Each reading you do will bring out another aspect or another view point. Note these down and add them to what you already know.

Keep your deck in a special place e.g. a box or wrapped in a special cloth. Take care of your deck as it may have to last you a while. Many wonderful decks go out of print and if it is your favorite, your muse, then you will be annoyed if you haven't looked after it.

Enjoy your new adventure!

The Major Arcana

The Fool
Card Number 0

The Fool is pictured as a young man setting off on a journey. He strides confidently into the unknown, which is usually represented as a path or road. Different decks use different symbols to represent the Fool's inability to understand the dangers present in the basic life forces around him. Some decks show the Fool actually stepping onto thin air, some have a fierce beast clawing at his trousers and in others he is pictured with his house built on the edge of a cliff.

The Fool's concerns are otherworldly; he is not governed by earthly pursuits. He is on a spiritual quest that will take him from birth to death; from innocence to enlightenment. He represents the spirit being born into a physical body. He has so much to learn, yet he is totally optimistic as he sets off on his quest. He senses that his journey is one of good, not evil, although he is unaware of the sorrows and difficult choices that await him.

The Fool is sometimes portrayed as a negative card; as one who behaves with foolishness, naivety and downright stupidity. These are certainly some of the pessimistic influences but it would be wrong to view the Fool as a negative card. We should view this card as we would the birth of a tiny baby who has all opportunities of the world ahead of him. We may fear for the child and hope that life is good to him, but we know he must travel his own road and make his own choices.

The Fool takes various ideas and dreams with him on his journey but he has not yet formulated a plan, or developed the perspective to put these ideas into solid, purposeful action. His expectations are high and he is ready for the challenges ahead; even though he has no clear idea of what these may be.

By the end of his quest he will have attained enlightenment in all areas of life. He will realize that his search for knowledge has been achieved and he will be ready to allow his spirit to be freed from his body.

Aspects to consider when the Fool is drawn:

- The possibility of fresh beginnings or changing to a different direction.
- The need for a person to accept that a time of major change and challenge lies ahead.
- The need to go back to basics and to let destiny reshape their life.
- The realization that it is a time of opportunity, when hope and excitement can lead them towards a new future.
- The presence of optimism which can transcend past difficulties and problems.
- The need to take a fresh look at surroundings, people or career and to lose the jaded feelings associated with age and familiarity. Try to see old problems in a fresh, enlightened way.

Negative influences of the Fool:

- Impulsiveness and naivety.
- Childish behavior.
- Bad decision making which hinders progress.
- Pig-headedness that rejects life forces outwith their experience.

When reading the Fool take great care not to frighten the inquirer or make them nervous about the challenges they will meet. Try to instill an excitement for a life about to change, and a hope for a brighter future.

The Fool can forecast changes in emotional life, work or lifestyle. The inquirer may partly be reacting to changes that are out with their control, yet it is important to emphasize the positive aspects of a new stage of their lives

The Fool is happy, trusting and open. Enjoy the Fool. Enjoy the excitement of stepping off a precipice into the unknown. Enjoy the vigor of youth.

The Magician
Card Number 1

The Magician card commonly shows a robed male figure standing in a sumptuous garden. There is a table in front of him on which lie the symbols of the four Minor Arcana suits: sword, pentacle (disc), cup and baton (wand). These symbols represent the four elements he uses to make his magic: air, earth, water and fire. His right hand is raised and he is holding a wand in it. His left hand points to the earth. The symbol for infinity, '∞', is above his head.

The Magician is the card of intellect combined with skill in order to accomplish a task. Without intellect the problem could not be attempted. Similarly, if the necessary practical skill was absent we would quickly grind to a halt. Whereas the Fool card can bring airy ideas and impulsive notions, the Magician grounds these ideas and takes them at least one step forward before they can drift away or disintegrate. It is this combination of wisdom and pragmatism that makes the Magician an excellent card to see in any spread.

The Magician has an air of intelligence and solemnity around him. He is skilled in his art and completely confident in his abilities. He is focused and contained. His 'magic' brings him acclaim but he is careful only to reveal the end result - never the work involved. But is it really 'magic' he performs, or rather is he a totally organized, quick-witted trickster? Does he use his speed of thought and sleight of hand to manipulate his audience into believing that simple mind tricks are actual magic? He is also a good communicator who can dazzle with his eloquence.

How then, do we read this card accurately? I believe this card is generally positive. It suggests that new skills, which can prove to be invaluable, can be learned. They may be life skills such as confidence, communication or simply learning to value oneself. They may be job or living skills such as computing or gardening, which give basic practical benefits to a life-style. These additional talents invariably lead to increased self-confidence and a willingness to take risks with new ideas. The combination of understanding and efficiency allows projects and business opportunities to bear fruit.

I call this the "boot up the backside" card. Its presence is sometimes to warn that the brain is not being sufficiently stimulated and that the person has succumbed to inertia and tedium. Stretch the mind and strive to accomplish chosen aims. The Magician tells us it is possible to harness ideas and energy and to apply them in a sound, efficient way.

Aspects to consider when the Magician is drawn:

- The need to combine intelligence and practical skills.
- The need to study or retrain to realize ambitions.
- The need to take the initiative and push forward.
- The need to communicate clearly to prevent misunderstandings.
- The need to take ideas and ambitions and to put them in motion using careful planning, skill and self-confidence.

Negative influences of the Magician:

- A wrong course of action may be taken because of trickery or cunning.
- Indecision can lead to under-achievement with a resulting drop in confidence.
- The person may be deluding themselves when they think they have the skills required to complete a project.

When reading the Magician it is vital to stress the need for balance between intellect and practical skills.

If the person is training, or learning a new skill, it is important to boost their confidence. They may be finding it hard to believe in themselves.

If the Magician is surrounded by a majority of Wands cards it suggests new skills will be learned through a career change.

The High Priestess
Card Number 2

The High Priestess card usually shows a composed, thoughtful woman sitting between two pillars. She has a moon on her headdress and rests her foot on a crescent moon She has a cross on her breast. She has a scroll, or a book, on her lap that she keeps half-hidden from prying eyes. Her eyes are wide and knowledgeable looking.

The High Priestess has wisdom that she can pass on, if requested to do so. However, the realm in which she acts is neither practical, nor earth-based. She holds the key to self-knowledge and to the inner-self. People who listen to her will recognize and understand who they really are. She offers the opportunity to delve into the psychic world; the chance to obtain answers by occult or paranormal means. She makes her decisions intuitively.

This is a very female card. It encapsulates the ancient ideas of the seer, or the wise woman. People ask her questions when more 'acceptable' methods of inquiry, such as science or religion, have failed them. Yet, she is an extremely important card in the modern-day. People are taking an increasingly jaundiced view of the world. They seem to be searching for understanding on a more intrinsic level. With the High Priestess, the answers come from within. She asks us to switch from our old, normally conventional, thought processes and let our imaginations have free rein. Enlightenment may arrive through dreams or by the use of psychic arts. The presence of the moon symbolizes the mystery and depths of knowledge that are available to us all if we take the chance to open our inner-selves to them.

While the capacity for this wisdom is within all of us, we should be prepared to acknowledge some hard truths about ourselves in the process of our inner journeys. The High Priestess does not always give direct answers. She can talk in riddles or set puzzles for us to solve. She can lead us to a solution, but it is only us that can discover a conclusive answer.

In daily life, the High Priestess may be someone who drives us on towards our goals. Their inspiration and enthusiasm can be a great help in the pursuit of our dreams.

The High Priestess is also connected with the world of science, particularly in a healing role such as alternative medicine. She stands for the positive influences of the paranormal, science and female intuition.

The negative qualities of the card show a rejection of the inner life and the single-minded pursuit of material or practical objectives. This can bring ultimate confusion and a loss of personal identity. It results in a lack of depth or an emptiness of character.

Aspects to consider when the High Priestess is drawn:

- The need to trust one's own intuitions when making decisions.
- The need to achieve an increased understanding of the inner-self.
- The need to abandon the old thought processes and structures that limit us.
- The need to set aside time for meditation and to let the imagination wander.
- The need to allow ourselves to be inspired and guided by others.

Negative influences of the High Priestess:

- Self-deception or deception by others.
- Superficial desires.
- Selfish pursuit of material gains, with no regard for others.
- Hidden influences attempting to cause chaos and destabilization.

When reading the High Priestess it is essential to emphasize that the most important source for the answers to life's questions is within ourselves. The inquirer may be ready to change the path that their life is following. Advise them to rely on their own intuition.

The Empress
Card Number 3

The Empress is generally depicted as a serene, apparently pregnant woman, seated on a throne in an abundant garden. Everything around her is bright, lush, well watered and blooming. Symbols of fertility and authority surround her. She has a crown of stars on her head. The figure of the Empress exudes femininity and gentleness.

Undoubtedly the Empress is the earth-mother; the representation of fertility, maternal care and female love. She is responsible for nurturing her children and is the focus for a happy family life. She has the power and esteem that her position merits and feels assured and esteemed in her role. The Empress is a wife, a mother and a true friend. She symbolizes pregnancy and a happy marriage.

The card also stands for fruitfulness, in thoughts and ideas. In her case she guarantees a tangible harvest or outcome; unlike the Magician. The reward may be through an increase in personal happiness or even involve additional wealth.

The negative aspects of the card come out when the power she holds overwhelms her caring, motherly instincts. This leads to manipulation, female domination and a scant regard for the needs and feelings of others.

Other, more basic, themes may involve infertility or an unwanted pregnancy.

In addition, creativity and practical insight can be replaced by sterility of thought and a lack of progression.

Aspects to consider when the Empress is drawn:

- A time of stability ahead.
- Ideas and creativity bringing projects to a happy conclusion.
- Fertility.
- Wealth and domestic stability.
- The need to open up and allow access to the more feminine side of our nature.

Negative influences of the Empress:

- Manipulation and misuse of maternal strength and power.
- Poverty in creative thoughts and actions.
- Sometimes infertility or unwanted pregnancy.
- Domestic chaos and financial instability.

The Empress it like a breath of fresh air in a spread.

It can sometimes be difficult to persuade someone that they can have stability, that nurturing is available to them and that they can look forward to a happy family life. Actually make them look at the card. Show them it is symbolic of the whole idea of maternal care and protection.

The Emperor
Card Number 4

The Emperor is pictured as a bearded, older man sitting on a throne. He is regal and serious-looking. He is surrounded by the symbols of his power; a mace, crown and orb. There is a river and mountains in the background, representing his dominion over the land. The Emperor's gaze can be described as somber, or even stern

The Emperor card signifies authority. It is a very male card and it incorporates the ideas of might and leadership. The Emperor is solemn, responsible and assertive; qualities he needs to rule his people. He is both respected and feared. He does not suffer fools gladly. He does have his fatherly side, but these gentler parts of his personality are kept under wraps most of the time. His thought processes are controlled. It sometimes takes him some time to reach a decision because of his fairness and his desire to ask advice from others including his High Priest and legal advisers. At other times he is dynamic, takes swift action and exercises his power aggressively.

The Emperor card urges us to be more assertive in our attempts to achieve our aims. Situations should be handled with authority and control. The card does not tolerate irresponsibility. Always think of the people who may be affected by your actions; be they family or work colleagues. Go forward with strength and confidence but do not trample over those in your path.

The Emperor is also a sign of authority in the form of governing bodies and the State. He represents corporate structures and major organizations and the controlling influences that these configurations can have on our lives.

There are two main negative aspects to the Emperor. The first is when he abuses his power resulting in tyranny and oppression. In personal life, this is manifested as intolerance and aggression. In wider society, it produces an organization or government that has scant regard for the suffering of its people. The other negative quality expressed in the Emperor is when his authority collapses. This causes a lack of respect and confidence leading to internal chaos for the individual or the State.

.Aspects to consider when the Emperor is drawn:

- The need to be assertive and to act with authority.
- The need to make controlled and well thought out decisions.
- The need to consider other people and, perhaps, put their interests first.
- The need to be aware of the 'bigger picture' (family, work, society) when reaching our conclusions.
- The need to accept the impending approach of order and stability in our lives.

Negative influences of the Emperor:

- Abuse of power and oppression.
- Indecision resulting in lack of confidence.
- Power struggles within organizations (e.g. work, government).
- Intolerance.
- Dislike of authority.

When reading the Emperor stress the assertive qualities of the card; particularly when advising a woman. This is not a card of remaining in the background and just blending in.

Approach situations with personal dignity and self-confidence.

Look for steady, not rapid, progress with the Emperor. Remember, there is a lot of inertia in corporate and governmental organizations.

The Hierophant
Card Number 5

The Hierophant is sometimes called the High Priest, or even the Pope. It usually shows a wise looking man sitting in a temple surrounded by followers who are listening intently to him. His right hand is held up as if to give a blessing. His left hand holds a staff. A pair of crossed keys are at his feet.

The Hierophant is a man of learning and understanding. He is respected and his advice is sought on matters of tradition and religion. He has faith in beliefs and ideas that have endured for centuries. He appears to have answers, although this may involve having faith or some kind of belief-system.

The Hierophant protects and sustains our heritage. He thinks that people - and society - need boundaries and laws by which they must live their lives. Within his beliefs, he teaches submission to divine laws and faith and he sees this as a way of maintaining the status quo.

The advice the Hierophant gives is practical and commendable but it is sometimes thought of as too simplistic for modern-day needs. The card can suggest that the person seeking answers needs to turn to organized religion in some way, or to approach life from a more spiritual angle. He promises good advice from someone in authority who can pass on learned information. This can include doctors, teachers or the clergy.

The Hierophant card also has links with both the teaching and religious vocations. It is symbolic of the search for knowledge and guidance and of the need to pass on these characteristics.

The negative aspects of the Hierophant appear when someone becomes indoctrinated by tradition or religion and they lose the ability to think things through for themselves. They become dogmatic and self-opinionated. They bar the door to any future developments by an over reliance on ideas from the past. Their narrow views on convention and normality become totally dominant.

The Hierophant also requires belief in principles that may not be relevant to modern-day life. This may cause conflict with, or a turning away from, orthodox religions. This can result in sadness and confusion for people who have believed in, and followed, their teachings.

.Aspects to consider when the Hierophant is drawn:

- The need to seek out the wisdom and knowledge of a respected and learned person.
- Perhaps the need to return to religion for guidance.
- The need to protect society and children by imposing clear rules and guidelines.
- The need to conform and fit in.
- The need to value tradition, old ideas and orthodox views.
- A need to teach, or to pass on wisdom through a calling.

Negative influences of the Hierophant:

- Indoctrination and obsession.
- Wrong or half-baked advice.
- Incomplete spiritual development by feeble-minded, unquestioning acceptance of ideas and teaching.
- Out-moded ideas or traditions that hold back people or society.

When reading the Hierophant be sympathetic to the religious and cultural traditions of the inquirer. Do not suggest that they should be more spiritual or religious. Alternatively, do not offend or alienate them by dismissing any beliefs that they may currently hold.

Encourage them to ask for, and to take, informed advice.

The Hierophant will generally give some kind of answer.

Homework for cards 0 to 5
Cards
0 The Fool
1 The Magician
2 The High Priestess
3 The Empress
4 The Emperor
5 The Hierophant / High Priest

Exercise 1

Take each card in turn. Place it in front of you. Relax. Take a few deep breaths. Touch the card. View the card from several different angles, noting the colors and the way that different parts of the card appear to be more prominent at different times.

For each card, really look at it for 2-3 minutes, and then answer the following questions.

(a) Does the card feel positive or negative?

(b) Write down the 6 adjectives that you feel best describes the card.

(c) Refer to the notes and explain, firstly, the positive influences of the card and then the negative influences.

For Fun:

(d) If the card had to be represented by a color, what would the color be? E.g. Magician - Yellow.

(e) If the card was to be represented by a film star, personality or place what would that be? E.g. The Fool - Jim Carrey.

Exercise 2

Answer the following two problems using the 3 card spread, i.e.

Past	*Present Course*	*Probable*
Influences	*of Action*	*Outcome*

(N.B. The people and problems are fictitious to you but try to answer intuitively and feel what the cards are trying to tell you.)

(a) A man in his early 20's feels stifled in his present job. Should he change course now, or is he better to wait for an opportunity to come up next year, due to a retirement?

The Magician   The Fool   The Hierophant

(b) A mother is worried about her teenage son's behavior. Advise her on how she should approach the situation.

The High Priestess   The Emperor   The Empress

The Lovers
Card Number 6

The card of the Lovers usually shows a naked man and woman in a sunlit, verdant garden. An angel has its arms outstretched above them. In the background, there is a serpent wound around an apple tree and the sun shines benevolently on them.

It is a beautiful card which, at first glance, looks happy and appealing. The Lovers themselves appear to be blessed by the angel and by the beauty and fertility of their environment. They are soul mates, made for one another by a generous god. Their needs in life are simple and neither their nakedness nor their intense love for each other embarrasses them. They have a strong bond between them; one built on trust and mutual attraction. They are not at odds with each other and seem harmonious and contented.

From this point of view, the Lovers is a good card. It indicates true love, emotional bonds and a meeting of hearts and minds. There is a physical attraction, even playfulness, about the card. It tends to suggest a deep relationship combined with commitment and familiar contentment.

A closer look at the card will reveal that everything in the garden may not be as rosy as it looked at first. The apple tree and serpent are suggestive of temptation. Is this the Garden of Eden, and is Eve about take the bait? Will the serpent divert Eve's eyes from Adam towards the forbidden fruit? She has a difficult choice to make and this is where the card's negative aspects start to become apparent. If a relationship is stale, the Lovers card implies that problems must be confronted and worked on. It also says that a person can choose to be in a relationship, or not. The angel may be observing, rather than blessing. It could be trying to guide the couple in their choices.

The Lovers is also the card of intuitive choice: and even second sight. It asks that we make choices with the heart, not the mind. It tells us always to trust our intuition, especially in love or relationship matters. Accept that our choice of partner may be out with our control. Much as we can plan for the perfect match, the person we end up being attracted to, or obsessed by, could be the complete opposite.

Aspects to consider when the Lovers is drawn:

- The need to follow our intuition, particularly with emotional concerns.
- That a committed, loving relationship is indicated.
- The need to trust a partner.
- A time of harmony and love.

Negative influences of the Lovers:

- Difficult decisions regarding relationships.
- Temptation - emotional or sexual - may cause disharmony and disruption in a relationship.
- A normally good partnership could face problems due to external factors.

When reading the Lovers be gentle with the inquirer as you are dealing with emotions.

Some people are very private and would not wish you to delve too deeply, especially if you sense dishonesty.

Remember. Never cast doubt on a relationship if that doubt is not there already.

The Chariot
Card Number 7

The Chariot is represented by a nobleman, dressed in armor, standing on a chariot which is being pulled along by two sphinx-like creatures. Over the chariot is a canopy of stars. The nobleman has a staff in his right hand. He appears to be in control, not only of the beasts in front, but of life itself.

The Chariot is a strong card. The figure looks assured, unafraid and totally confident in himself. With this self-belief, and with his sturdy chariot, you feel that all problems and obstacles will be crushed and overcome. Victory will be his and he can face the world in the knowledge that he has performed well, and lived up to expectations.

So, the Chariot is a very positive card; one which promises victory through effort and mastery of the problems of life. Progress is guaranteed though willpower and self-confidence. Success will surely follow. It is a time to move ahead, put plans into motion and be confident in outcomes. It is also the card of good health with energy. It shows that the physical body is strong enough to cope with the demands placed upon it.

The Chariot is also the card of travel and transport and can signify increased mobility. In addition, it is the card of ambition, which sets events in motion, leading to ultimate success.

The negative aspects of the Chariot normally come through a lack of control or willpower. This can result in breakdown, loss of ambition and defeat. If a person has continually been thwarted in their attempts to battle life's obstacles it will be difficult to carry on being hopeful and strong. This is especially true if the problems are health related. Despite this, it is important for them to somehow pick themselves up and try once more.

Aspects to consider when the Chariot is drawn:

- The need to put effort into conquering difficulties.
- The need to keep the light of ambition burning brightly.

- The need to realize that, although outside influences may stall us, they can eventually be overcome.
- Good health, with increased energy levels.
- Progress through self-confidence and self-control.
- Travel and transportation links.

Negative influences of the Chariot:

- Loss of control when under pressure.
- Lack of self-belief and self-confidence.
- Health problems taking over life.
- Panic and chaos.
- Progress, or even transport, delayed.

When reading the Chariot, stress the need for perseverance and self-belief. Sometimes, if there seems to be a never-ending stream of problems, a person can be at the end of their tether. They may not have the energy for one more effort. Yet, try to convince them that the Chariot signifies confidence and determination, leading to eventual success.

Strength
Card Number 8
The card of Strength shows a young woman pulling open a beast's mouth. She is controlling the beast by sheer force and determination. Her face is serene; even though she is in great danger. She seems to be convinced that she will win the struggle in the end.

If we are to understand the meaning of the card, we must accept that life has a habit of burdening us with negative events and, sometimes, catastrophes. We can either give in to these happenings and go under, or we can take the advice of the card, and bear them with acceptance and determination.

Strength is a card that asks us to have faith, to fight against our misfortunes, to treat negative life events as a challenge and to control fear and weakness.

In some decks Strength is known as Desire. This brings in a more sexual aspect to the card. We are asked to be aware of human impulses and physical desires and we are urged to control them. It warns against excess in various areas of pleasure including alcohol, sex and the pursuit of material gain.

Control, balance and the need for perseverance are the very essence of the card.

Aspects to consider when Strength is drawn:

- The need to have strength and fortitude to help overcome negative events.
- The need to battle with a health problem.
- The need to believe in oneself, without over-indulging the ego.
- The need to have spiritual strength to overcome dark thoughts.
- The need to control passion and desire.
- The need to have self-discipline and self-reliance.
- The need for courage in adversity.

Negative influences of Strength:

- Weakness and self-doubt.
- Lust and obsession running riot.
- No willpower to overcome ill-health.
- Uncontrolled ego.
- Emotional hysteria.

When reading Strength it is important to reassure the inquirer that they can cope with negative events. But, this is not a card which gives quick answers. For most of the time, there will be daily battles with adversity and only time, and a calm determination to succeed, will produce the necessary results.

Be careful and tread very cautiously if you sense a sexual or obsession aspect to this card. The inquirer may already be aware of this aspect but they may not appreciate it being pointed out to them.

The Hermit
Card Number 9

The Hermit generally shows an old, bearded man in a monk's habit. He stands alone, in a barren wasteland. His head is bowed; his eyes closed. He holds a staff in his left hand and holds aloft a brightly lit lantern in his right.

The Hermit looks to be very still and self-contained. In this desolate landscape we would probably be uncomfortable and perhaps a little scared, but he seems calm and unaware of his surroundings. His countenance is peaceful and accepting, with an inner strength and tranquility. He gives the impression that he could maintain his stance indefinitely, without the need of material comfort or outside interference. He has gained much wisdom and self-knowledge.

The Hermit can indicate the need to retreat from the grind of daily life to enjoy solitude. It is only by quietly analyzing our lives that we come to understand the truth of our circumstances; who we are and why we are here. We need time to evaluate, ponder and to take stock. Introspection allows hidden thoughts and deep feelings to come to the surface.

The Hermit carries the light of truth and can suggest that someone is either searching for a truth, or that a truth will be revealed to them by subsequent events. They will then have to face the facts and heed the advice that is given.

This card can also ask that wisdom is gained and decisions thought out carefully before taking any action. The quest for wisdom may be either spiritual or practical, and there may be someone who will act as a guide on this search.

The Hermit also shows that the power of thought can overcome physical constraints. Just think of those people walking over hot coals or lying on a bed of nails.

Negative aspects of the card include withdrawal; both from personal responsibilities and from society. Good advice will not be taken and warnings ignored. Someone who has been content to be left alone can easily become isolated and lonely. The Hermit shows someone hiding from the truths of life; be it emotional life or even work.

Aspects to consider when the Hermit is drawn:

- The need to look inwards.
- The need for solitude, even isolation.
- That it is time to re-evaluate life and to face facts, even the difficult ones.
- That great wisdom can be achieved through the use of self-discipline.
- The difference between being alone and being lonely.

Negative influences of the Hermit:

- Withdrawal from responsibilities.
- Ignored advice leading to problems.
- Loneliness.
- Introversion, self-obsession and self-preoccupation.

When reading the Hermit, emphasize the need to make time for oneself, whether you are a successful businessperson or a busy parent.

Life decisions should be made only after a period spent finding out what are the real facts of a situation and then carefully assessing the pros and cons. In addition, take notice of what it could mean to that particular individual and their special circumstances.

The Wheel of Fortune
Card Number 10

The Wheel of Fortune card usually features a man and a woman perched on top of a large wheel. The wheel is being turned by the hand of Fate. They are both wearing crowns. The man is holding a large goblet. The woman looks as though she is clasping tightly to the man. A figure is seen falling from the wheel.

The Wheel of Fortune brings it home to us that, however much we may plan for the future or try to control our destiny, events sometimes force us in a different direction. Depending on the turn of the wheel, it may mean good luck or bad luck. The figures on the wheel represent ourselves. At any moment, the wheel could turn, sending us off on another path which may change our destiny forever. Obviously, we need to be open, and to trust in fate, in order to be able to reap any rewards.

The Wheel of Fortune can bring a change of fortune; for better or worse. It can also be deceptive since what initially may look to be bad luck may, in the long term, turn out to be a blessing in disguise. Karmic influences may be at work. The consequences of past decisions may need to be faced. In fact, bad luck may be considered to be Karmic retribution. In the long-term the turn of the wheel affects us fairly, although it may be hard to accept this. It can be difficult to believe that fate brings us good and bad luck in equal measure.

Generally, the Wheel of Fortune heralds change and the unfolding of a new stage of our destiny. A new life cycle is about to begin, with all the excitement, pleasure and, maybe, nervousness that change can bring. This is a time for flexibility and openness; a time to be carried along on the crest of wave.

At times, the change may leave us feeling out of control and frightened. The only way to deal with this is to have trust in what the Fates have in store for us.

The Wheel of Fortune normally brings a good outcome, but this may have to be considered over a long time period. Relax, and enjoy the feeling that you are being influenced by Fate and that the outcome will, eventually, be in your favor.

Aspects to consider when the Wheel of Fortune is drawn:

- The need to trust fate and allow changes to take place without resistance.
- A change of luck, for better or worse.
- A new life cycle, bringing gains and improvements.
- Taking the longer term view when considering the effects of change.
- The need to accept, and enjoy, good fortune.
- Karmic influences.

Negative influences of the Wheel of Fortune:

- Bad luck causing despair.
- Fertile ideas being overwhelmed by bad luck.
- A turn for the worse.
- An unwillingness to adapt to change.
- Fragility of life.

When reading the Wheel of Fortune remember that destiny is influenced by outside events. Plans and ambitions may falter because of bad luck; or they may thrive when the wheel turns in a more advantageous direction.

Try to reassure the inquirer that, although they may not be in complete control, this may be beneficial.

We have all been touched by amazing coincidences that have led to better things:- lovers meeting on a train; being in just the right place, at the right time; chance meetings with people who then greatly affect our lives. These are governed by the Wheel of Fortune.

Homework for cards 6 to 10

  Cards

  6 The Lovers

  7 The Chariot

  8 Strength

  9 The Hermit

  10 The Wheel of Fortune

Exercise 1

Repeat Exercise 1 in the previous section for the above 5 cards.

Exercise 2

Repeat Exercise 2 for the following questions:

(a) A woman's relationship is causing her concern; she feels there is no longer a future for her and her partner. Can you advise?

Past Influences	*Present Course of Action*	*Probable Outcome*

The Chariot   The Lovers   Strength

(b) An elderly man has had health worries. He fears for the future and does not want to be a burden on his family. Can you help him?

The Hermit   The Wheel of Fortune   The Chariot

(c) A young couple have been trying for a baby for a year. They are now worried about infertility. What should they do?

The Empress   The High Priest   The Wheel of Fortune

Justice
Card Number 11

Justice shows a regal woman seated on a throne-like chair. She holds a sword in her right hand and a set of scales in her left. She looks serious yet benevolent. The sword signifies decisive action while the scales provide balance and fairness.

Justice is a primary human need. We need to know, and trust, that the bad things in life are offset by good parts; that injustice served upon us will not go unpunished; that good will overcome evil. When Justice is drawn in a spread it shows that it is a time to be fair and honest. You must not deceive, even unintentionally. It is an indication that you must examine the whole picture before reaching balanced conclusions that may not necessarily be in your favor. Treat people with fairness and compassion.

In some of the newer decks, Justice is called Karma. This gives the promise that, in time, wrongs will be righted and evil will be visited upon those who commit evil deeds. Sometimes justice is not seen to be done even in one's lifetime. A belief in Karma allows us to accept that eventually justice *will* be done.

Justice invariably requires truth, sincerity and a belief in humanity. It is one of the most essential attributes for a civilized society. The card of Justice was sometimes seen as swift and merciless but, over time, it has softened and now has a more moderate character.

In practical terms, Justice can also indicate legalities such as divorce, marriages, business contracts and house moves. In spreads relating to the world of work, it can suggest the need to deal honestly with workmates, to take care with contracts or even arbitration. In all of the above there must be decency, equality and trust.

As a positive card, Justice promises a good and fair outcome. Balance is restored to life and equality and integrity wins the day.

The negative aspects of Justice can include bias, or delays in justice being done. Contracts may be deceptive. Treaties or promises can be broken. The legal system itself may seem unfair and not in tune with the feelings of society. There may be prejudice because of someone's gender, color or religion. When the card is negative, it is vital to be strong and to fight the injustice, not just for oneself but for the sake of society as a whole.

Aspects to consider when Justice is drawn:

- The need to believe that the scales will not be loaded against you and that fair play will be done.
- The need to go through a legal process for various important life-events, such as divorce, self-employment and moving house.
- The need to be fair and thoughtful when dealing with people.
- The need to accept that a more balanced, less fraught time lies ahead.

Negative influences of Justice:

- Inequality and unfairness.
- Prejudice and bigotry.
- Legal complications and delays.
- Broken promises.

When reading Justice, it is important to view the other cards in the spread carefully. It may not be relevant in terms of legalities or finances, but it may very well be significant to an inquirer's unbalanced emotional life. It may show an imbalance of mood or a lack of self-worth. The keys are always balance and fairness. If necessary, point out that being fair is not to be confused with being soft on others and allowing them to take liberties.

The Hanged Man
Card Number 12

The Hanged Man card shows a young man suspended upside down from a tree. He hangs by one foot only. His other foot is tucked behind his straight leg. His hands are in the small of the back - they may be bound or simply placed there. A halo surrounds his head. His expression is one of calm acceptance.

This card always causes a stir when it appears, not least because the inquirer thinks it is upside down! Also, the image of a young man dangling from a beam or tree makes it look like quite a bad card. Most people would not want to find themselves in his position. But take a close look at the card. The man's face is serene and accepting; he is not struggling or in any distress. He obviously has a clear insight into his situation and accepts it. He may see that this time of inactivity is necessary for future progression or he may feel that the sacrifice he is making just now is worth it for the beliefs he holds.

The halo around the Hanged Man's head gives us some under-standing of this aspect of sacrifice linked with the card. It implies martyrdom, or some kind of act that is for the greater good. The young man might be taking a stand for some cause or for some one precious to him. He feels that any discomfort or delay he must endure is justified if he can maintain his convictions or makes life better for someone close to him. Crudely speaking, he believes the probable gain is worth the possible pain.

The other main aspect of the Hanged Man is the basic inertia of the card. He is going nowhere, at least for the moment. His life is on hold and he is unable to make progress. It seems as if he is at the mercy of the whims and decisions of others. Although this is certainly negative, but his face *is* tranquil, showing he under-stands his predicament. He accepts the delays and the lack of movement. He is prepared to wait on the correct signals or answers before he struggles to free himself from the ties that stop him getting on with his life.

Aspects to consider when The Hanged Man is drawn:

- The need to sacrifice oneself for a strong belief.
- The need to put other people first.
- The need to accept current constraints in order to enjoy future benefits.
- The need to accept delay and a temporary halt in life's progress.
- The need to remember that wisdom can sometimes come though hardship.

Negative influences of The Hanged Man:

- Sacrifices going on too long making life unbearable.
- The refusal to accept delays or constraints which can lead to impulsiveness and rash decisions.
- Selfishness and a lack of concern for society.
- Inertia turning into a long-term problem, e.g. unemployment.
- A fear of looking inwards to find wisdom.

Remember when reading The Hanged Man to stress the need to take time to ensure that all the facts are clear before decisions are made. The inquirer may be full of enthusiasm for a plan, a new venture or a relationship. Try to slow them down and advise against impulsiveness. It may be that the situation is right but that the timing is wrong.

Death
Card Number 13
Death is pictured as a skeleton wearing armor or a long black cloak. He sometimes holds a banner with the symbol of a rose and he normally holds a scythe. He rides through the land on horseback and seems indiscriminate in his choices. He is feared

and people kneel in front of him awaiting their fate. The sun is shown setting in the distance.

Arguably, Death is the most confusing card in the Tarot deck. It looks so menacing and frightening, but is probably one of the most benevolent and exciting cards. In our culture, death is feared and regarded as something that should be kept hidden away and not talked about. Elsewhere, however, death is seen as just a natural part of life. The act of dying and the funeral service can be treated as a celebration of the start of a new existence for the deceased. This is surely the lesson we must take from this card. It rarely signifies physical death. It is more of an end to an outmoded way of life that is no longer relevant to us.

The Death card symbolizes the need to break with the past and to enter a fresh, exciting phase in life. It asks that we do not cling to obsolete ideas and that we face the new challenges and move forward. Death indicates that life is about to change substantially, and that the inquirer will need to have energy and determination to see the end result. The old life could be a relationship that has gone stale, a job that has ceased to excite our imagination or even emotional ties to the past which are now holding us back.

The card asks us to accept personal transformation and renewal. The change may be sudden, but it will still need to be acknowledged and acted on. Sometimes the necessary action may seem ruthless, but sometimes - as the old saying goes - you have to be cruel to be kind.

Aspects to consider when Death is drawn:

- The need to accept change and to act accordingly.
- The need to take a leap of faith into your future.
- Looking at the future in a new light and to leave out-of-date ideas in the past.
- The need to sort out old problems quickly and efficiently; then move on.

- The need to overcome a fear of change.

Negative influences of Death:

- Refusing to accept change and stay stuck in the same old rut.
- Irreversible life changes that we cannot cope with because they arrive too suddenly, e.g. redundancy, bereavement, sudden ill-health, etc.
- Stagnation and the death of the spirit.

When reading Death remember that the inquirer may not be prepared for the changes the card promises. Try to instill a feeling of confidence in the future and a feeling of excitement for the challenges and changes which lie ahead.

Temperance
Card Number 14
The card of Temperance shows an angel standing in beautiful surroundings, a clear, blue pond with flowers around it. The sun shines brightly though hills in the background. The angel looks peaceful and composed with its eyes closed. It is pouring water from a goblet in one hand to a second goblet in the other hand. The card exudes a sense of calm and poise.

Temperance certainly looks very pleasant and is welcome in a spread where a person's life is in a state of upheaval or change. It is an optimistic card which promises a way out of difficult times or stress. It certainly asks us to look forward to a time where we have both stability and security around us; a time when we can contemplate the future from a position of equilibrium. Temperance represents maturity and clear thought. Decisions will be taken with foresight and good management. Opposing forces will be balanced and Yin and Yang restored to harmony. Extreme personality traits or impulsive notions will be held in check. This is a very healing card, allowing old wounds to heal over and be forgotten.

In some of the newer decks, Temperance is called Time and this highlights the need for patience. Only time will tell with this card. Problems can be solved but only with the passage of time. This is often difficult to accept, but, like Strength, Patience is a virtue.

Negative aspects of Temperance come usually though impatience or having an outlook that is not balanced. With a lack of balance, people are prone to weakness and they can resort to extreme measures to try to fulfill their needs. This can be manifested in conditions such as alcoholism, bulimia, anorexia or even self-mutilation. Similarly, impatience can cause poor judgment, impulsive behavior or a failure to adapt to the constraints of everyday life.

Aspects to consider when Temperance is drawn:

- The need for patience; wait and see.
- The need for good management and co-operation.
- The need for a more balanced outlook.
- The need to believe that it is a time for harmony and healing.
- The need for maturity when it comes to making decisions.

Negative influences of Temperance:

- Lack of balance in life leading to extremes of behavior.
- Impatience and impulsiveness.
- Poor judgment and immaturity.

Remember that, in most circumstances, Temperance is a good card but it can be hard to get across the main aspects of patience and balance to an inquirer who wants to dash through life and does not want to slow down. Stress that life has to go at its own pace and should not be forced forward.

The Devil
Card Number 15

The Devil shows a creature who is half man, half beast, the Horned God. He has bats' wings and his face, although basically human, has animal characteristics. He perches on a stone, to which are chained two naked humans. These male and female figures also have horns and tails. The Devil holds a lighted torch in one hand and the other is raised. He stares menacingly.

The Devil looks like a destructive and oppressive card. It is dark and fearsome. It is difficult to see it as a good card, unless it is viewed as a warning against evil, a helpful gesture to alert the inquirer to the negative aspects around them.

Undoubtedly the Devil card is an indication that something is seriously wrong with one's life. This can be external negative influences or those dark depths of human nature that would normally be dormant or kept well under control. In fact, the need to control negative human tendencies is, perhaps, the very essence of the card. The Devil can represent aggression, envy, selfishness and an obsession for material wealth and power. It can also suggest that a person has undergone great change due to their longings or addictions. Temptation towards the darker side of life can lead to chaos and a loss of self-respect. Once the Devil wins it is extremely difficult to break free again. This is symbolized by the human figures enslaved by his chains.

There can also be a very carnal side to the Devil card. It can be a warning of sexual fixation, or lust. An inquirer may feel out of their depth with the strengths of their desires and their physical need for another person. This can lead to further potential difficulties due to deception, lies and chaos in a normally stable life. Yet, this card can be difficult to control and some people will succumb to temptation, no matter how dire the potential consequences. This is a side of human nature which we normally avoid delving into too deeply.

Viewed as a warning, the Devil card asks us to seriously look inside our souls and to yield not to temptation.

Aspects to consider when The Devil is drawn:

- The need to be aware of deception, or problems, relevant to work, health or relationships.
- The need to confront fears that keep us bound to an oppressed way of life.
- The need to overcome strong, dangerous desires whether sexual, material or addictive.
- The need to control basic animal instincts including lust, aggression, irrational fear and persecution.

The Devil is a negative card and at extremes it can lead to:

- Addiction problems. Alcohol, drugs, eating disorders.
- Sexual infidelity.
- Abuses of power including bullying and harassment.
- Discounting other people in a blinkered pursuance of material gain.

It is important to be sensitive when The Devil appears in a spread. If you sense a sexual or addictive aspect, be terribly careful. You can easily get out of your depth and flounder badly. Do what you can to allow the inquirer to bring the problem out into the open themselves.

Homework for cards 11 to 15
Cards
11 Justice
12 The Hanged Man
13 Death
14 Temperance
15 The Devil

Exercise 1

Repeat Exercise 1 in first section for the above 5 cards.

Exercise 2

Repeat Exercise 2 in first section for the following questions:

(a) A woman has been married 8 years and has a young family. She is attracted to a man she met through a friend. She feels there is something special between them and wants to know if she should go with her feelings and have an affair. What do you advise?

Past Influences	Present Course of Action	Probable Outcome
The Devil	Temperance	Death

(b) A taxi driver is afraid of losing his driving license. He stupidly had a few drinks at Christmas and then drove. What do you see happening? The case against him has been delayed twice.

The Hanged Man   Justice   The Devil

The Tower
Card Number 16

This card shows a tower being struck by lightning with such force that fires break out and the battlements are split. A man and a woman are seen falling from the tower into the gorge below. The Tower is dark, manic and destructive. In older decks it is sometimes referred to as "The Lunatic Falling from the Asylum".

The card has a dark and negative appearance. In one split second, this solid looking structure has been wrecked and destroyed. The people inside have either been knocked off by a powerful force, or have been compelled to jump to try to save themselves. They are falling at great speed and have fear and terror etched on their faces.

Fate, in the form of the bolt of lightning, has suddenly and irrevocably changed the lives of the people who lived in the tower. Their home is ruined and their future looks precarious to say the least, with little hope of regaining what they have lost. This is probably the essence of the card; dramatic changes meaning that we can never go back to the old ways of life. It is very significant that the change is sudden. There is no way of anticipating, or preparing for, the forthcoming changes.

In real life, the Tower brings chaos and disturbance after the existing way of life has been overthrown. It can result in disruption, conflict and destruction leading to crisis.. Yet the Tower does have the effect of reducing us to the basics in life. Once the fire has been extinguished the bricks to build a new tower will still be there; a phoenix can arise from the ashes. Fate may seem to have landed a severe blow but we are still able to pick ourselves up and begin again. The falling figures can survive, even if, perhaps temporarily, their bodies are damaged. They have the opportunity of a different, possibly easier, path to follow in life.

The Tower is still viewed as a negative card mainly because people are instinctively scared of sudden change that is out with their control. The only positive qualities are the chance to rebuild their lives in a better way or the chance to redefine their future.

Aspects to consider when the Tower is drawn:

- Sudden, major change out with control e.g. redundancy, accidents, emotional rejection.
- Unplanned change of job or residence.
- Unexpected setbacks or shocking change.
- Conflict and destruction.

- Aggression and tyranny.
- Following the upset and destruction, a new path can appear which will lead us to a different way of life.

When reading the Tower, try not to scare the inquirer, the card looks fearsome enough. Stress the regenerative possibilities associated with the card.

The Star
Card Number 17

The Star card shows a naked young woman who is pouring water from a goblet in each hand. She pours one onto the earth, the other into a clear pool. The sky is bright blue and dominated by a large yellow star which has several smaller white stars surrounding it.

The Star is a very positive card which exudes brightness, clarity and openness. It gives rise to feelings of hope and optimism for the future and promises a time of peace, calm and serenity. In spreads that are dominated by doubt and seemingly insurmountable difficulties, it is a very welcome sight. It pledges a better time ahead and the ability to have clearer insights to problems. All the person has to do is to hold on to their hope and optimism and life will reward them. A new cycle of life is about to begin with spiritual renewal and an increase in confidence. In health-based spreads, it indicates an improvement in the future quality of life.

The few negative aspects of the card tend to present themselves when a person refuses to contemplate the future with nothing more than a jaded, defeatist viewpoint. There is also an unwillingness to adjust to change, missed opportunities and a pessimism, which other people find unattractive and off-putting. There will always be doom and gloom merchants but, sometimes the Star card can change even their dismal outlook. Just when you think it will never happen, an old grouch can become enthusiastic and inspired.

Aspects to consider when the Star is drawn:

- The fulfillment of hopes and dreams following a time of doubt.
- Optimism and inspiration.
- Light at the end of the tunnel.
- Clear insight into problems.
- Confidence and vigor.

Negative influences of the Star:

- Defeatism.
- Unwillingness to adapt to challenges.
- Missed opportunities.

With the Star, instill a sense of hope and optimism for the future. Guide and advise the inquirer to allow themselves to be open to opportunity when it comes knocking.

The Moon
Card Number 18

The Moon ordinarily shows two dogs, or wolves, baying at the moon. It is normally in dark colors with black and grays dominant. The moon itself is bright but it casts ominous shadows over two towers in the background. A lobster-like creature emerges from the depths of an opaque pool. This card always appears sinister, dark and eerie.

The Moon seems to have two distinct aspects. Firstly, it covers the way the card is associated with the psychic world. The full moon shining in the darkness is a symbol of the need for humans to explore that side of their nature which seems to be unknown or unknowable. It implies embarking on a quest into the world of intuition and dreams. The card can indicate that the inquirer needs to search for answers from their spiritual side, rather than looking at the questions on a strictly intellectual basis.. They should be made aware that dreams may be a source of premonitions and that they should begin to analyze them accordingly. The Moon tends to be chosen by people who work in professions which involve creativity, imagination or flights of fancy.

The Moon's second major aspect is related to a darker, more dangerous side. Complete darkness brings fear and threats. Never doubt that hidden dangers, monsters and terrors lurk in the darkness. Should we try to confront these fears and dangers, the light from the moon will give us some help at least. The fears may be phobias or, more likely, a dread of negative feelings, such as anger and the dark side of nature. Many people will not analyze the causes of their anger and fear. This is because they may have to encounter a part of themselves that has lain buried for a long time.

The moon controls the tides and asks us "to go with the flow" of life rather than struggling, particularly in times of tension, fear and depression. This does not mean do nothing. It intends that, even if we find life hard, we should make the most of what happiness is available.

Aspects to consider when the Moon is drawn:

- The need to face fears and to delve into the unknown.
- Acceptance that flights of the imagination and daydreams are basic human needs.
- Depression and anxiety are the mind's way of dealing with underlying problems. Confront the problem and physical illnesses and mental distress may vanish.
- Do not suppress the desire to understand the unknown, or to fulfill ambitions that may appear crazy or unattainable.
- Always respond to intuitions and gut-feelings. They will serve you well.
- Accept life's ebbs and flows with good grace.

Negative influences of the Moon:

- Despair and lethargy.
- Unseen illnesses out with your control.
- Deception, lies and an inability to face the truth.
- Daydreaming instead of action, when life is tedious or problematic.
- Depression - a serious health problem.

When reading the Moon be aware that the inquirer may be feeling low and possibly overwhelmed by feelings of despair. They may also be confused by their own actions and they may want definite answers.

They must be given the support and encouragement to make their own decisions. Never tell an inquirer what to do. They could take your (possibly inaccurate) advice to extremes, with drastic consequences.

The Sun
Card Number 19

The Sun card normally shows two children in a garden full of flowers and greenery. The children are healthy and happy. They show the energy and vitality of youth. A bright, benevolent sun shines down on them. They appear to living a charmed and happy life full of celebration and abundance.

The Sun is a pleasant and warm card. It brings success and achievement and is a positive influence in any spread. It promises growth and development in all areas of life. It is particularly important when it is drawn along with health cards, as it is a sure sign of better health and increased energy to come. This can mean an end to depression, anxiety or stress disorders, or simply just a boost to general well-being which can make pain or long-term illness more bearable.

In business or work, the Sun brings success, achievement and a realization of ambitions or goals. It is also a good financial card promising a fruitful harvest or rewards for the effort expended.

It is also the card of favorable relationships, where love and commitment transcend the day to day troubles of life. The rewards implied by the Sun may be more of a spiritual rather than physical nature. Important points to remember about this card are childlike happiness, innocent pleasures and an ability to enjoy the simple things.

Obviously, as with all cards, there are good and bad influences to the Sun. The negative ones in this case are few. One is that any improvement in health may only be temporary. The card can also suggest allergies or uncommon illnesses. Any pleasure or happiness promised may also be tinged with some sadness. It can mean that any success may be short-lived. However, the Sun is much more positive than negative, and it should be viewed as a good omen in most spreads. It can also be the card of twins! Watch out when combined with the Empress!

Aspects to consider when the Sun is drawn:

- Improved health; increased energy.
- Financial success or success in work.
- Pleasure and satisfaction from realizing a vocation.
- A time of happiness and achievement.
- Development of a warm and caring relationship.
- Happiness with love life, family life or friendships.

Negative influences of the Sun:

- Happiness tinged with sadness.
- Too much emphasis on material success.
- Feelings of emptiness despite reaching desired goals.
- Only temporary respite from health problems.
- Broken contracts relating to work or relationships.

With the Sun, it is important to read the surrounding cards. This card can reduce the effect of other negative influences and promise happiness following a tough time. If placed in a spread with a majority of Swords, it can signal the light at the end of the tunnel. When it is found in a majority of mundane Pentacles it can "lift" the daily grind to a brighter, more acceptable level. The Sun is a very happy card, full of promise and hope for a brighter future.

Judgment
Card Number 20

The card of Judgment shows the archangel Gabriel blowing his trumpet from on high, calling the dead to rise from their graves on the Day of Judgment. It is an auspicious card which signifies a call from heaven to come along and enjoy a new existence with their Maker.

The Judgment card implies a connection with the future, of a new life that is about to begin, bringing all the hope and excitement that a fresh start can bring. Yet, it can be a very spiritual card and, if people are looking for practical solutions, it can sometimes be a problem to read. The ideas of resurrection, spiritual awakening and the connection with the divine can be a little bit airy-fairy for many pragmatic people. It is important, however, that this aspect of the card is well understood. When Judgment is drawn it shows that the inquirer is reaching a stage in their life where they will have a truer understanding of themselves and of how they fit into life; they can see the 'bigger picture'. Hidden aspects, unclear direction and wasted opportunities are a thing of the past. They are reborn with the understanding and acceptance that only comes with experiencing all the ups and downs of life. An alternative name for Judgment is Revelation, which emphasizes the more spiritual aspects of the card.

In more practical terms, Judgment suggests the completion of one stage of life, energies replenished and confidence in the future. The inquirer is content to leave what has gone by in the past where it belongs. They are prepared to accept what is to come and will be able to adapt to the new patterns of life. The have, in effect, changed from the inside out.

One other quality that Judgment draws on, is that of compassion and forgiveness. The dead have been resurrected, having atoned for any misdeeds in the past. They go forward into the future with pure souls.

Aspects to consider when Judgment is drawn:

- Renewal and progress are only possible once the past has been laid to rest.
- A time of major change is ahead where important life decisions will be made.
- Renewed energy and trust in what lies ahead.
- The need to seek forgiveness and to make up for past wrongdoing.
- A grasp of the bigger picture and of one's purpose in life.

Negative influences of Judgment:

- Rejecting a new way of life; looking backward instead of forward.
- Pig-headedness and refusing to seek forgiveness.
- Fear of the unknown; drawing back from opportunity.
- Stress the renewal aspect of Judgment. Anyone *can* change, *if* they accept the proper guidance. By accepting some blame or responsibility, feuds can be healed and bridges mended.

The World
Card Number 21
The World is pictured as a naked female with a scarf draped around her body. She is dancing, apparently in mid-air, inside a

laurel wreath. She holds a baton in each hand. She appears contented, happy and full of vitality. There are images of a man, an eagle, a lion and a bull; one in each of the four corners of the card. The card is sometimes called the Universe.

The World is the last of the Major Arcana cards and represents the completion of life's journey. The Fool card stands for the birth of the spirit into the physical body to travel life's path which will be full of obstacles and challenges. The World card shows that all that can be learned on this journey has been acquired and that the spirit has rejoined the ether and found its way back to the Divine.

The laurel wreath represents the fact that life has come full circle. Knowledge, enlightenment and spiritual awareness have been achieved though this rite of passage. There is the sense of fulfillment, conclusion and success. The spirit has been healed and has prevailed over its restraints.

The World is one of the most beneficial cards in the entire Tarot deck. In a practical sense, it signifies satisfaction, contentment with past decisions and the idea of freedom. Accomplishments are noted and it is a time of personal gain; in status, finances or emotional concerns. The card says "Yes" to future potential and promises victory in those challenges yet to come. Take pleasure from present and future success. Things will fall into place. Enjoy!

It is also the card of perfection and triumph. Life will be much happier, with cares and woes left in the past. The World promises happy marriages, emotional satisfaction and a greater understanding of the self.

Aspects to consider when the World is drawn:

- Completion and fulfillment.
- Promise of reward and gratification.
- Overcoming past difficulties and an increase in prosperity.
- The end of an era and the start of a new life cycle.
- Infinite future potential.

Negative influences of the World:

- Completion held up; temporary delay to the start of a new life cycle.
- Feelings of discontent and lack of fulfillment.

The World is a very positive card and is a joy to see in a spread. Try to pass on the feeling of contentment for the beginning of a new life cycle.

Homework cards 16 to 21

Cards

16 The Tower
17 The Star
18 The Moon
19 The Sun
20 Judgment
21 The World

Exercise 1

Repeat Exercise 1 in previous section for the above 6 cards.

Exercise 2

Repeat Exercise 2 in previous section for the following questions:

(a) A difficult situation has arisen between neighbors who, although they used to get on all right, had a fight following a party. Certain religious differences turned into bigotry. They now ignore each other and are both upset and confused. Advise.

The Moon   Judgment   The Tower

(b) A teenage girl is really worried about her brother. Unknown to their parents, he is experimenting with drugs with a school friend. What should she do?

The Tower   The Moon   The Star

(c) A young Asian girl is having her marriage arranged by her parents, who she loves unconditionally. She is, however, quite westernized and would like to know if her parents will make a good choice for her.

The Sun   The Star   The World

Occupations Suggested by the Major Arcana

This is partly from my own experience over many years and also for fun. Look at your cards: see what you feel and see if it matches up. Then use this knowledge for further inquirers.

Card Number Card Name Occupations

0 Fool Advertising; Risk Investment; Self-Employed

1 Magician Student; Skilled Tradesmen e.g. Joiner, Electrician; Communications Industry

2 High Priestess Science and Technology; Clairvoyant; New Age Field e.g. Aroma therapist, Reiki

3 Empress Nursing; Social Work; Gynecologist; Full-Time Mum, midwife. carer.

4 Emperor Banking; Corporate Industry; Politician; Police Force; military.

5 Hierophant Teaching; Clergy; Telephone Helpline; Citizens' Advice; Samaritans

6 Lovers Dating Agency; Counseling Services; Stock Market; Jewelers; escorts;

7 Chariot Transport Workers e.g. Taxi Drivers, HGV Drivers, Train Drivers, etc. riding instructor; PR.

8 Strength Builders; Heavy Plant Workers; Gym Workers; Athletes; extreme sports; managers.

9 Hermit Home Workers; Mathematicians; Researchers; home business; monks and nuns.

10 Wheel of Fortune Gaming Industry - including Bookmakers; risk assessors; insolvency practitioners; trapeze artists

11 Justice Lawyers; Court Officers; Prison Officers; Arbitrators; Police; weight advisors.

12 Hanged Man Steeple Jacks; Miners; Oil Rig Workers; long term investors.

13 Death Undertakers; Armed Forces; Hairdressers; life counselors.

14 Temperance Negotiators; Stress Management Counselors; Personnel Officers; Human resource management.

15 Devil Vets; Double Glazing Salesman; Sex Industry; bankers

16 Tower Mental Health Workers - including Psychotherapists; Insurance Workers; demolition workers.

17 Star Satellite System Workers; Astrologers; Sailors; Fishermen; performers; map makers.

18 Moon Writers; Actors; Entertainers; Night-Shift Workers; mystics.

19 Sun Health Workers; Doctors; Those Working Abroad; travel advisors; meteorologists.

20 Judgment Musicians; Social Workers; Family Therapists; Housing Officials; judges;

21 The World Civil Servants; Multi-National Corporations; Internet Workers; Town Planning

The Minor Arcana

The Minor Arcana is made up of four suits, each with 14 cards. The suits are known as Wands (or Batons), Cups, Swords and Pentacles (or Coins or Discs). Each of the four suits represents a different aspect of life:

Cups:	Emotions; Matters of the Heart
Swords:	The Intellectual Mind; Mental Aspects
Wands:	The Higher Mind; Personal Fulfillment; Career
Pentacles:	The Practical Life; Finances; Life-Style

Each suit has an associated element.

Cups:	Water
Swords:	Air
Wands:	Fire
Pentacles:	Earth

- Cups and Pentacles are regarded as female suits.
- Swords and Wands are regarded as male suits.
- Each suit also governs three astrological signs.

Cups:	Pisces, Cancer, Scorpio - (Water signs)
Swords:	Gemini, Libra, Aquarius - (Air signs)
Batons:	Leo, Aries, Sagittarius - (Fire signs)
Pentacles:	Taurus, Capricorn, Virgo - (Earth signs)

Each suit is made up of 10, numbered, Small cards and 4 Court cards. The Small cards represent events while the Court cards represent people, as follows:

Pages:	Children or young adults
Knights:	Men and women in their 20's or 30's
Queens:	Mature women
Kings:	Mature men

For example, a mature woman who is a water sign would be the Queen of Cups and a young child who is an earth sign, would be the Page of Pentacles.

Some decks suggest that Knights simply portray males but in my experience they describe either sex. If Pages and Knights were just male, then that would be unbalanced. Some decks have Princesses and Princes instead of pages and knights and the Knights become the traditional Kings! (It is quite romantic to pair the Knight with the Queen instead of the King, as a king never fought for his queen...the champion knight did!)

I prefer to read the court cards as representing people. Some readers use them to signify events but I feel there are enough card meanings in the suit without adding this to the court cards .If you can really understand the court cards as people, it can give you an indication of how those people can be affecting the client and the problem. It can also do your reputation no harm when you can identify e.g. that the page of cups is a water sign daughter who is giving her mum a hard time in the context of the spread. One of the first things I look for is the court cards and how they are placed in the spread and what affect they are having. In a spread where the question is about love, a queen surrounded by two kings should give you a big clue as to what the problem might be! You can then identify them by star signs and give greater clarity

Always remember that I would like you to *feel* whether the card is positive or negative rather than using reversals

The Suit of Cups

Points to remember when reading Cups:

1. Emotional life is not just love life, so do not limit it to this. Love is just one emotion; hate, envy, sadness and terror may be equally appropriate.

2. Treat the inquirer with kid-gloves if Cups are underpinned by a subsidiary Swords suit. They may be mentally fragile.

ACE OF CUPS
Positive Aspects
~ A fresh start emotionally.
~ Fertility and birth.
~ A new insight into emotional problems.
~ A new project beginning.

Negative Aspects
~ The need for a fresh start, in emotional matters.
~ A compelling desire for a child where fertility is uncertain, or when the timing is simply not right.

The Ace of Cups is normally a very positive card which brings contentment, love and creativity

TWO OF CUPS
Positive Aspects
~ A new romance or friendship.
~ Partnerships of all kinds; including business ones.
~ The sharing of ideas and creative thoughts.
~ Enjoyment and fun.

Negative Aspects
~ A broken partnership including separation and divorce.
~ Possible unfaithfulness.

The Two of Cups is normally a positive card. It epitomizes all the excitement and hope at the start of a relationship. A joyful and bonded card.

THREE OF CUPS

Positive Aspects

- ~ Health and energy.
- ~ Emotional reasons to celebrate, possibly a birth.
- ~ A time to celebrate life; to give ourselves a little treat.
- ~ Female friendship

Negative Aspects

- ~ Self-indulgence and self-congratulation.
- ~ Smugness and selfishness.

This is normally a positive card. It encapsulates fun, dancing, sexuality and abandon.

FOUR OF CUPS

Positive Aspects

- ~ The need to re-evaluate an emotional life which has grown stale.
- ~ Seek out new horizons.

Negative Aspects

- ~ Dissatisfaction with life.
- ~ Boredom and inertia.
- ~ Despair and despondency over life-style.

The Four of Cups is normally a negative card. It symbolizes feelings of being trapped, bored and insufficiently stimulated, particularly with regard to relationships.

FIVE OF CUPS

Positive Aspects

- ~ The ability to see people as they really are; including the good and bad bits.

Negative Aspects

- ~ Worry and regret.
- ~ Broken engagements; broken promises.
- ~ Negative events coming out of the blue.

This is usually a very negative card signifying some kind of emotional loss. Regret, disappointment and sometimes anger all surround this card

SIX OF CUPS
Positive Aspects
- ~ Childhood and childish pursuits.
- ~ Happy family life with the focus on children.
- ~ Harmony and fulfillment.
- ~ Happy memories.

Negative Aspects
- ~ The need for less structure and more fun.

The Six of Cups is normally a very positive card. It sums up all the pleasant aspects of childhood; fun, freedom, security and summer.

SEVEN OF CUPS
Positive Aspects
- ~ Possibly none.

Negative Aspects
- ~ Having to choose between too many opportunities.
- ~ Too much of a 'good' thing.
- ~ Dissatisfaction with life, despite outward appearances.
- ~ Sleep disturbances.
- ~ Possibly losing a firm grasp of reality.

The Seven of Cups is invariably a negative card. It shows that life is often not what it seems and that financial and material success may disguise unhappiness.

EIGHT OF CUPS
Positive Aspects
- ~ The need to turn away from the establishment and to break free.
- ~ An emotional turning point which can provide greater

freedom and the opportunity to discover a sense of the true self.

Negative Aspects

~ Recklessness and impulsiveness.

~ Running away from problems rather than facing up to them.

The Eight of Cups can either be positive or negative, depending on the effects that result from breaking free.

Simple Five Card Spread

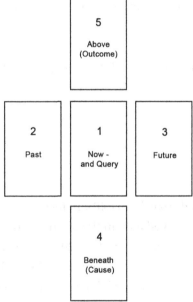

1 Represents the current position and what the question is

2 Represents what has led up to the present situation

3 Represents the future and what action should be taken

4 Represents the obstacles to the desired outcome

5 Represents the answer, or outcome

Homework
Cards
Ace of Cups — Eight of Cups (8 cards)

Exercise 1
For each of the above 8 cards, thoroughly inspect it, then really look at it for 2-3 minutes and answer the following questions.

(a) Does the card feel positive or negative?
(b) Write down 6 adjectives that you feel best describe the card.
(c) List the positive and negative aspects of each card.

Exercise 2
Answer the following questions using the Simple Five Card spread, i.e.:

```
    5
2   1   3
    4
```

(a) A married man in his 40's is feeling lost and unfocused. He has achieved a lot in life but he is still not satisfied. His relationship with his wife of 20 years seems boring and he feels that they are no longer in love. Both his children have left the parental home and he wonders what he should do next. Advise.

5. The Sun
2. The Magician   **1.** 4 of Cups   **3.** 2 of Cups
4. The Devil

(b) A young man has finally made the decision to tell his family that he is gay. He fears his father's reaction most, but he feels he needs to be honest. He would also like his family to meet his new partner. Advise.

	5. The Tower	
2. Ace of Cups	1. 7 of Cups	3. The Hierophant
	4. The Emperor	

The Suit of Cups (continued)

NINE OF CUPS

Positive Aspects

- ~ Success; especially on a material level.
- ~ Good, robust health.
- ~ Satisfaction with the outcome of endeavors.

Negative Aspects

- ~ Self-indulgence and self-congratulation.
- ~ Using hospitality to boast about lifestyle.

The Nine of Cups is usually a positive card that suggests it is a time to sit back and enjoy the fruits of your efforts.

TEN OF CUPS

Positive Aspects

- ~ Long-term happiness.
- ~ Security within a loving caring family.
- ~ Lasting friendship and emotional well being.
- ~ Happy celebrations

Negative Aspects

- ~ Family life that can stifle and control.
- ~ Loss of friendship; or a friendship turns out to be false.

The Ten of Cups is normally positive. It is a culmination of all the happy Cup cards and it brings happiness, security and joy.

The Court Cards

The court cards of the suit of cups are associated with the water sign i.e. Pisces, Cancer and Scorpio.

PAGE OF CUPS
Positive Aspects
~ This child, or young adult, is normally a caring, sensitive person. They are dreamers and can be very artistic. The Page can open us up to new and exciting changes if we were only to follow his, or her, open, child-like example.

Negative Aspects
~ The Page can also represent the kind of dreamer who achieves little. They can be selfish and self-indulgent. Or too naive for real life.

KNIGHT OF CUPS
Positive Aspects
~ The Knight can represent someone who is intelligent and who likes to be liked. They can bring great opportunity for progression and can excite others to follow their dreams. They are both romantic and idealists.

Negative Aspects
~ The Knight can also depict someone who uses their emotional intelligence to trick people, or lie to them. They can be a fake; all sweetness and light on the outside but very dark in their heart.

QUEEN OF CUPS
Positive Aspects
~ The Queen can represent a very intuitive woman who is loving and affectionate to family and friends. She can pick up on moods and emotions and cares deeply about those who love her. She has a tendency to daydream and can have very psychic dreams.

Negative Aspects
~ The Queen can also stand for a manipulative woman who

can be very intense and hysterical when things do not go as planned. She can be scathing and uncaring about people who are not in her inner circle of family and friends. The epitome of the 'pushy' mum!

KING OF CUPS
Positive Aspects
~ The King can symbolize a kind, caring man who concentrates his efforts in finding solutions to problems. He is a skilled negotiator who brings maturity and knowledge to any unbalanced situation. He is the loving patriarch, the gentle advisor.

Negative Aspects
~ The King can also be a skilled fraudster who uses his position in life for his own personal gain. He can be the emotionally abusive father who uses fear to get his own way.

You may have noticed that I have not said whether the individual Court cards are normally positive or negative. This can only become clear when the surrounding cards are read and this also includes the situation in which the Court card itself is found. People can be the cause of predicaments. They can be in the middle of a situation and they may even be responsible for resolving one. Read the surrounding cards!

Homework
Cards
Nine of Cups — King of Cups (6 cards)

Exercise 1
For each of the above 6 cards, thoroughly inspect it, then really look at it for 2-3 minutes and answer the following questions:

(a) Write down 6 adjectives that you feel best describe the card.

(b) List the positive and negative aspects of each card.

(c) Does the card feel positive or negative? - *Ignore Court Cards.*

Exercise 2

Answer the following questions using the Simple Five card spread:

(a) A young man walks nervously through the door. He says he has never had a reading before but that he is really mixed up. He got engaged last year after dating for 6 months. He was beginning to feel trapped and was about to call it off when his fiancée announced that she was pregnant. He is terrified about the responsibility and is confused over whether he loves her or not. Advise.

	5. King of Cups	
2. The Devil	**1. The Tower**	3. Ace of Cups
	4. 5 of Cups	

(b) A mother is seriously worried about her nineteen-year-old daughter. She does not know if she is mentally ill or dabbling in drugs but she feels her behavior is bordering on the extreme. Advise.

	5. Knight of Cups	
2. 9 of Cups	**1. Temperance**	3. 8 of Cups
	4. The Devil	

The Suit of Wands

Points to remember when reading Wands:

1. The suit governs the aspect of personal fulfillment. This can be through career, work or labors of love.

2. It is associated with the element of fire and represents the Fire signs of the Zodiac, i.e. Leo, Aries and Sagittarius.

ACE OF WANDS
Positive Aspects
~ Chance for a fresh start within a career.
~ The beginning of a new enterprise or project.
~ The need to grasp opportunities with confidence.
~ The need for an aggressive and determined approach to a problem.

Negative Aspects
~ Missed opportunities.
~ Lack of innovation or inspiration.
~ Infertility - both physically (male) and of ideas.

The Ace of Wands is normally a positive card encompassing the very male aspects of the suit, e.g. motivation, confidence, assertiveness (possibly tinged with aggression).

TWO OF WANDS
Positive Aspects
~ Wealth and success as a result of hard work.
~ Prosperity through self-belief and focused energy.
~ Relates mainly to material wealth, e.g. car.

Negative Aspects
~ Pride before a fall.
~ Abusing wealth for dubious purposes, e.g. power, domination or self-promotion.

The Two of Wands is usually a positive card that can reassure the inquirer that hard work will pay off in financial and materialistic ways.

THREE OF WANDS
Positive Aspects
- ~ Success, from luck or good fortune.
- ~ Partnerships or groups bring success.
- ~ New opportunities arising from previous success.

Negative Aspects
- ~ Turning your back on help or assistance.
- ~ Stubbornness or denial causing missed opportunities.

The Three of Wand can be both positive and negative as the inquirer may gain success through accepting help or assistance or, equally, they may turn down these offers of support and forge ahead in their own way and still achieve the success they deserve.

FOUR OF WANDS
Positive Aspects
- ~ Celebrating the completion of a project.
- ~ Peace of mind after a period of hard work.
- ~ Fun and revelry surrounding a job well done.
- ~ Romance and pleasure.

Negative Aspects
- ~ The calm before the storm.
- ~ The need for a respite from physical labors.

This is generally a joyful, celebratory card. Imagine the scene from the film "Witness", with Harrison Ford, where the Amish community have all worked together to build a house and are now feasting and celebrating among themselves. That, surely, is the Four of Wands.

FIVE OF WANDS
Positive Aspects
- ~ None.

Negative Aspects
- ~ Obstacles and personal battles obstructing progress.
- ~ Petty aggravations and general upheaval.

~ Strife and opposition.

The Five of Wands is usually a very negative card which can leave the inquirer feeling tired and low because of all the obstacles in their day to day lives.

SIX OF WANDS

Positive Aspects

~ Victory and success.

~ Good progress through hard work.

~ Gaining what is rightfully yours.

Negative Aspects

~ Few - except, perhaps, possible delays regarding the above.

The Six of Wands is normally a positive card suggesting success and fulfillment.

SEVEN OF WANDS

Positive Aspects

~ The need to act with courage and valor when confronting enemies or problems.

~ Banish negative thoughts   → "Go for it!"

Negative Aspects

~ Adversity and powerful opposition threatening a way of life.

~ Giving in to opposition without a proper fight.

The Seven of Wands is generally a negative card. It emphasizes the need to fight oppression, to seriously stand up against enemies and to have courage for the struggle.

EIGHT OF WANDS

Positive Aspects

~ The need to grab opportunity and make swift progress.

~ The need to hurry things along to a completion.

~ Communications and news bringing hope for a sudden

change.

Negative Aspects

~ Impulsive action resulting in chaos.

~ Sometimes, sudden dismissal or redundancy.

The Eight of Wands is normally a positive card bringing good news. The card advises moving with haste towards accomplishment.

Colette's 10 Card Spread

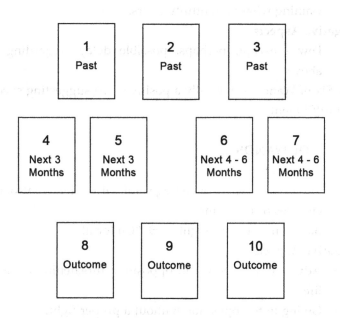

1, 2, 3 Represent the past
4, 5 Represent what is ahead for the next three months
6, 7 Represent what is ahead for the next four to six months
8, 9, 10 Represent the final outcome or longer term events

This is the first spread so far that will really give you the opportunity for linking card meanings. No card should be read in isolation and using this will allow for you to 'put two and two together' as such. The past cards should be read as a 'lead up' to the issue, and the outcome cards as the merged conclusion of influences. The monthly cards show a progression of stages between the lead up and the outcome. I use this spread constantly for business clients.

Homework
Cards
Ace of Wands — Eight of Wands (8 cards)

Exercise 1
For each of the above 8 cards, thoroughly inspect it, then really look at it for 2-3 minutes and answer the following questions.

- (a) Does the card feel positive or negative?
- (b) Write down 6 adjectives that you feel best describe the card.
- (c) List the positive and negative aspects of each card.

Exercise 2
Answer the following question using Colette's 10-card spread, i.e.:

```
1     2     3
4 , 5       6 , 7
8     9     10
```

- (a) A young woman has been given a great opportunity for promotion within her company. Until this came along she and her husband had been trying for a family for the last 12 months, without success. She now does not know whether to take the job, which involves a lot of stress and traveling, or to be contented and continue to try for a baby. Can you advise?

1. Page of Cups   2. The Magician   3. Knight of Cups
4. The Fool,   6. Ten of Cups,
   5. Five of Wands   7. The Empress
8. The Tower   9. Three of Cups   10. The Star

The Suit of Wands (continued)

NINE OF WANDS
Positive Aspects

~ Stability and security after a time of battle.
~ Opposition overcome with future plans and growth assured.
~ Good health after a time of struggle.

Negative Aspects

~ A chink in the armor leading to a defeat.
~ Security threatened by a personal problem or lack of forethought.

The Nine of Wands is normally a very positive card that indicates stability and security and a determined effort to maintain a lifestyle.

TEN OF WANDS
Positive Aspects

~ Success beyond all hopes and dreams.
~ Good fortune and resultant wealth.

Negative Aspects

~ The personal price of success, e.g. less time for family and friends.
~ Refusal to delegate work or authority.

The Ten of Wands is usually a positive card that brings success, recognition and stability. Yet it can be truly negative when the demands outweigh the benefits. Caution the inquirer to beware.

PAGE OF WANDS
Positive Aspects
~ This can represent a young, ambitious person who is quick to respond to change and is enthusiastic in all they do. They can be fiery and emotional but still fun to have around. They are natural born leaders and quick to assume this role.

Negative Aspects
~ It can also signify a more superficial person who seeks self-promotion and who could well overstep the mark in the pursuit of their ambitions. If the card represents a child, it can show boisterousness and hyper activity and lack of concentration.

KNIGHT OF WANDS
Positive Aspects
~ This can stand for someone who delights in challenges and action. They are ready to move quickly and seize all opportunities. They are risk takers or entrepreneurs. They may have to make quick decisions regarding travel, work and job changes as well as the home, including house-moves.

Negative Aspects
~ Can be someone who enjoys stirring up trouble. They are not content when life is quiet and uneventful. This card comes out often for powerful business people and life's risk takers.

QUEEN OF WANDS
Positive Aspects
~ This may be a practical woman who is not afraid to speak her mind and who is ambitious for her family. She regards success as her family's right and is prepared to work hard for it. She is very hard working and may have high expectations.

Negative Aspects

~ May turn out to be a very domineering person herself who has a tendency to overwhelm her children with her strong opinions. She may expect robust health for both herself and in others. This can make her intolerant of health issues or lack of direction in others.

KING OF WANDS
Positive Aspects

~ This can signify a traditional, secure man who has achieved fulfillment and success. He is loyal and caring. He seeks happiness through his family and can also be relied upon to sort out problems. He may be pleased with all aspects of life but especially in areas relating to work and career.

Negative Aspects

~ He may be prejudiced against change or anything that threatens the status quo. His self belief may not be shared by others and he can be a bully both physically and intellectually.

Homework

Cards

Nine of Wands — King of Wands (6 cards)

Exercise 1

For each of the above 6 cards, thoroughly inspect it, then really look at it for 2-3 minutes and answer the following questions:

(a) Does the card feel positive or negative? (Ignore court cards)

(b) Write down 6 adjectives that you feel best describe the card.

(c) List the positive and negative aspects of each card.

Exercise 2

Answer the following question using Colette's 10-card spread, i.e.:

1	2	3
4 , 5		6 , 7
8	9	10

(a) A 55-year-old man is considering early retirement. His health is good and he would like some time to himself. Both his sons are directors of his company but they are still young and he worries about leaving them to cope. He has worked hard to establish his company as one of the country's top exporters of glassware. What should he do?

1. The Hierophant	2. Two of Wands	3. Ten of Wands
4. The Magician		6. King of Wands
5. Justice		7. Nine of Cups
8. Temperance	9. Page of Wands	10. The Devil

The Suit of Pentacles

Points to remember when reading Pentacles:

1. The Suit of Pentacles represents the material aspects of our lives, i.e. the Practicalities of Life.

2. It is sometimes called the mundane suit that covers environment, finances and the way we live our lives on a day-to-day basis.

3. Where the majority suit is Pentacles, look for a subsidiary back-up, e.g. do finances have an effect on relationships (Cups), or job satisfaction (Wands)?

4. It is associated with the element of earth and represents the earth signs of the Zodiac, i.e. Taurus, Capricorn and Virgo.

ACE OF PENTACLES
Positive Aspects
- ~ A new beginning in finances or environment, e.g. house move.
- ~ Material gain.
- ~ A change in circumstances leading to increased material comfort.

Negative Aspects
- ~ Over-emphasis on the importance of material objects.
- ~ Greed

The Ace of Pentacles is normally a very positive card that brings excitement about a change for the better.

TWO OF PENTACLES
Positive Aspects
- ~ As a warning: avoid buying on credit. Only spend what you can afford. Budget carefully.

Negative Aspects
- ~ Take care with established businesses.
- ~ The need to perform a balancing act with money or the practicalities of life, e.g. a working mother try to cope with a job *and* running a house.

The Two of Pentacles is usually a negative card warning against imbalance in finances, life's practical aspects or even in a working environment.

THREE OF PENTACLES
Positive Aspects
- ~ Business opportunities.
- ~ Effort rewarded with material success.
- ~ Discussions about business projects.

Negative Aspects
- ~ Missed opportunities due to inertia or fear.
- ~ Constant effort for no reward.

The Three of Pentacles is normally a positive card indicating financial rewards in return for hard work.

FOUR OF PENTACLES
Positive Aspects
- ~ Stability through finances accruing.
- ~ Real, or apparent, increase in status. May be via promotion, or by the acquisition of the symbols of power such as fast car, mobile phone or modern office.

Negative Aspects
- ~ Abuse of power and position.
- ~ Meanness.
- ~ Fear of delegating in case someone shows themselves to be capable.

This is generally a positive card indicating an increase in power. It becomes negative when the power is abused or a fear that it will be taken away again.

FIVE OF PENTACLES
Positive Aspects
- ~ None

Negative Aspects
- ~ Loss of financial stability, position or power.
- ~ Financial struggles.
- ~ Sometimes, infertility or barrenness.

The Five of Pentacles is always a negative card indicating a loss of stability or a reduced standard of living. Consider the wider picture with this card including the effect on emotions, ego and health.

SIX OF PENTACLES
Positive Aspects
- ~ Using financial good luck to assist others.
- ~ Financial stability allowing for some of life's extras including the freedom to donate time and money to charity.

Negative Aspects
- ~ Financial gain attracting hangers-on or possible theft.

The Six of Pentacles is usually a positive card. It emphasizes the need to spread your good fortune around a little. This may be in the form of charitable work or by rewarding workers.

SEVEN OF PENTACLES
Positive Aspects
- ~ None

Negative Aspects
- ~ Lack of interest in employment resulting in boredom and possible isolation.
- ~ Dwelling on opportunities missed in the past.
- ~ Inertia due to being in the wrong job or position.

The Seven of Pentacles is a negative card which indicates boredom, stagnation and a "couldn't care less" attitude. Obviously, changes need to be made.

EIGHT OF PENTACLES
Positive Aspects
- ~ Steady gains as a result of hard work.
- ~ Prudence, including investments and savings for a rainy day.
- ~ Small gains from varied sources, e.g. tax rebates, back pay etc.

Negative Aspects
- ~ Becoming a workaholic to try and increase living standards.

The Eight of Pentacles is normally a positive card suggesting stability in the work place with steady pay. It is a very practical and grounded card; mundane, but comfortable.

The Yearly Spread

```
         1
      2    3
    4   5    6
    7   8    9
 10   11    12
        13
```

This is a general spread for a general reading for the year ahead. I have also seen this run as a circle with the first card at top.

Card 1 represents on the 1st of the next calendar month e.g. Sitting date = 21st May: then Card 1 = June; Card 2 = July; Card 3 = August, etc.

Examine the card for each month and tell the inquirer the major influences of card, e.g. emotional, financial, mental or career.

Check for the patterns that appear in the spread, e.g. two or three similar cards in successive months.

Look for a dominant suit to provide the major influences for the year, e.g. will emotions or practicalities dominate it.

Enjoy picking out months with celebrations in them.

Remember that sad cards can depict anniversaries of sad events, e.g. bereavements.

Card 13 is the resolution card and indicates how the inquirer will feel about the year.

Homework

Cards

Ace of Pentacles — Eight of Pentacles (8 cards)

Exercise 1

For each of the above 8 cards, thoroughly inspect it, then really look at it for 2-3 minutes and answer the following questions.

    (a) Does the card feel positive or negative?

    (b) Write down 6 adjectives that you feel best describe the card.

    (c) List the positive and negative aspects of each card.

Exercise 2

Answer the following question using the yearly spread.

    (a) A woman in her late 30's wants a general reading. She is with a group of women on a girls' night out and does not have any questions. She has not been for a Tarot reading before. The date is 21st May.

1. The Sun
2. Two of Pentacles
3. Three of Cups
4. The Emperor
5. Five of Wands
6. Ten of Wands
7. The Star
8. Five of Pentacles
9. The Lovers
10. Four of Cups
11. Ten of Cups
12. Page of Cups
13. Temperance

The Suit of Pentacles (continued)

NINE OF PENTACLES
Positive Aspects
- ~ Secure material life allowing emotional and mental rewards.
- ~ The pleasures of wealth.
- ~ Also, the card of unearned income, e.g. inheritance, winnings.

Negative Aspects
- ~ An apparently good lifestyle achieved by underhand means, e.g. the drug baron in his mock Tudor house.

The Nine of Pentacles is normally a positive card indicating pleasure from wealth in terms of emotional and time concerns.

TEN OF PENTACLES
Positive Aspects
- ~ Prosperity and wealth.
- ~ Attaining wealth through business or inheritance.
- ~ Contentment with the practicalities of life, e.g. house, business and finances.

Negative Aspects
- ~ The burdens of wealth or financial success including employees, tax, accountants and lawyers.
- ~ Family squabbles over money, even wills.

The Ten of Pentacles is usually a positive card but can be negative depending on the inquirer's frame of mind. At times they can accept the strains of business success while, at other times, it threatens to overwhelm them.

PAGE OF PENTACLES
Positive Aspects
- ~ In terms of a person, the Page of Pentacles can represent a student, particularly one who is studying a practical

subject, such as accounting. They can be kind and practical and a very helpful person to know!

Negative Aspects

~ The Page may also symbolize someone who is mean, too meticulous and far too obsessed with practicalities. He may be unemotional and obsessed with deadlines and material things.

KNIGHT OF PENTACLES
Positive Aspects

~ This card can stand for someone who is patient and hardworking. They may not be an intellectual, but they are definitely skilled. They may excel at a detailed trade. Emotionally they may pursue a potential partner over along time.

Negative Aspects

~ Someone who may be too timid too take risks. They can be indecisive and appear to be slow. Their energy may be frustrating and heavy and they can be moaners.

QUEEN OF PENTACLES
Positive Aspects

~ Contentment with their home life. Someone who is very grounded and down to earth. She can give good practical advice and be very a shrewd businesswoman. An excellent home manager or administrator.

Negative Aspects

~ This queen can be discontented even when she has a good lifestyle. She can be overly concerned with material gain or pleasure. She may be emotionally bankrupt.

KING OF PENTACLES
Positive Aspects

~ The King of Pentacles may be a man who is practical,

reliable and solid. He may be slow to anger but is certainly not afraid of a business confrontation or unable to assert his position.

Negative Aspects

~ He may be too structured an opinionated. In business he may wield some power but commands little respect. This king can be stubborn and will be in it for the long term. He is not a quitter, which can lead to his downfall.

Homework

Cards

Nine of Pentacles — King of Pentacles (6 cards)

Exercise 1

For each of the above 6 cards, thoroughly inspect it, then really look at it for 2-3 minutes and answer the following questions.

(a) Does the card feel positive or negative? (Ignore court cards)

(b) Write down 6 adjectives that you feel best describe the card.

(c) List the positive and negative aspects of each card. Ignore court cards.

Exercise 2

Answer the following question using the yearly spread.

```
         1
     2       3
   4    5    6
   7    8    9
  10   11   12
        13
```

(a) A man in his 40's wants a business reading. He appears confident and affluent. During the first five minutes his mobile phone rings but he is not embarrassed and takes the call using a good three minutes of your time. He smiles, turning on the charm. Proceed. The date is August 16th.

1. Knight of Pentacles   **7.** Four of Cups
2. Three of Pentacles   **8.** The Devil
3. Nine of Pentacles   **9.** The Moon
4. Two of Wands   **10.** Temperance
5. The Emperor   **11.** Strength
6. The Lovers   **12.** The Sun
13. King of Pentacles

The Suit of Swords
Points to remember when reading Swords:

1. This suit represents the rational mind, or the intellect.

2. It governs the way we approach life on a mental or cerebral level.

3. Swords are becoming more common in today's stressful lifestyles, but try to isolate a subsidiary majority in order to ground the reading.

4. It is associated with the element of air and represents the air signs of the Zodiac, i.e. Gemini, Libra and Aquarius.

ACE OF SWORDS
Positive Aspects
  ~ The willpower to change stagnant attitudes.
  ~ Breakthrough, victory and success achieved by force of character.

~ Clear insight into problems and the ability to produce swift solutions.

~ The need to have a single-minded, perhaps ruthless, approach.

Negative Aspects

~ Misuse of power.

~ The use of mental aggression or bullying to achieve aims.

The Ace of Swords is normally a positive card that brings forced change for the better. It may simply reflect a rude awakening, where a person faces up to the facts of life for the first time.

TWO OF SWORDS

Positive Aspects

~ The card of truce and compromise.

~ The restoration of harmony and balance, possibly following some kind of trauma.

~ Protection via the presence of a personal belief system.

Negative Aspects

~ Sometimes reflects misplaced trust which can lead someone along the wrong path, e.g. some type of cult.

The Two of Swords is usually a positive card, but only for a short time. Compromises and cease-fires can only be tolerated in short bursts. Eventually there will be losses of control and the breaking of trusts.

THREE OF SWORDS

Positive Aspects

~ None.

Negative Aspects

~ Sorrow and heartbreak.

~ Tears deriving from loss or separation.

~ Limited progression from previous times of sorrow, e.g. Bereavement.

The Three of Swords is truly a negative card where the heart is wounded and may never recover.

FOUR OF SWORDS
Positive Aspects
~ Convalescence or hospitalization resulting in recovery from illness or stress.
~ The need for personal retreat or solitude.
~ Relief from daily stress or anxiety.

Negative Aspects
~ Enforced solitude or isolation, perhaps due to physical causes.
~ Can even be rejection due to psychological disorders.
~ Ostracism.

This is can be a positive card, if the inquirer is prepared to take it as an omen, warning against stress and intolerable responsibilities.

FIVE OF SWORDS
Positive Aspects
~ None.

Negative Aspects
~ Failure or defeat.
~ Loss, through cowardice or lack of willpower.
~ Succumbing to negative thinking.
~ Giving up on something before you have really started.

The Five of Swords is a negative card. It indicates a subjugated mental attitude and gives us the eternal victim.

SIX OF SWORDS
Positive Aspects
~ Success after a time of trouble.
~ The need to move forward without looking back over your shoulder.
~ Long journeys resulting in fresh hope; sometimes

emigration.

Negative Aspects
- ~ A hasty retreat that brings only temporary relief.
- ~ Sometimes the difficult job of leaving loved ones behind.

The Six of Swords is normally a positive card but sometimes it can be difficult to start the journey as so many things can anchor us to the past.

SEVEN OF SWORDS
Positive Aspects
- ~ None.

Negative Aspects
- ~ The need for secrecy or stealth.
- ~ Sometimes the need for concealment relating a job change or escape from a relationship.
- ~ A degree of restlessness within someone.
- ~ Possible risks resulting from past decisions.

The Seven of Swords is another negative card. The inquirer may be restless and testing their limitations. Warn them that they should be cautious and secretive or risk ruining their present situation, e.g. job, marriage, etc.

EIGHT OF SWORDS
Positive Aspects
- ~ None.

Negative Aspects
- ~ Enforced isolation as a result of life events, e.g. redundancy, bereavement, friends or family moving away, etc.
- ~ Sometimes harassment for being different, e.g. race or sex.
- ~ Mental regression into a dream-like state to escape pain.

The Eight of Swords is a negative card. It signals isolation, intolerance and restrictions. The inquirer may be unaware of the reason behind their punishment.

The Twenty One Card Spread

For examining a single problem in depth

1 2 3 4 5 6 7 ----- PAST

8 9 10 11 12 13 14 ----- PRESENT

15 16 17 18 19 20 21 ----- FUTURE

The inquirer shuffles and cuts the cards while concentrating on their problem. Deal off the top 21 cards in the above pattern. Interpret each section, Past, Present and Future, by studying individual cards, groups of cards, dominance of certain suits etc. this will really test your ability to connect card meanings and not read cards in isolation.

Homework
  Cards
  Ace of Swords — Eight of Swords (8 cards)

Exercise 1
For each of the above 8 cards, thoroughly inspect it, then really look at it for 2-3 minutes and answer the following questions.

(a) Does the card feel positive or negative?
(b) Write down 6 adjectives that you feel best describe the card.
(c) List the positive and negative aspects of each card.

Exercise 2
Answer the following question using the 21 Card Spread, i.e.:

1	2	3	4	5	6	7	PAST
8	9	10	11	12	13	14	PRESENT
15	16	17	18	19	20	21	FUTURE

I want you to do this for real with your own decks. Shuffle your cards and concentrate on the question. Answer according to what you see and feel.

A woman in her 20's wishes a problem-solving reading. She was very close to both her parents until her Dad died two years ago. She did not cope well at all, and, for unknown reasons, rejected her Mum. Her Mum was devastated but, with time, has recovered. The daughter has just heard that her Mum is to remarry but she has not been invited.

Will she ever get her Mum's trust back? Will she be forgiven? How should she approach the situation?

The Suit of Swords (continued)

NINE OF SWORDS
Positive Aspects
~ None
Negative Aspects
~ Depression and suffering.
~ Violence, fear and loss.
~ Dreams and premonitions of bad events; even the death of a loved one.
~ In extreme cases, it can be a card warning of potential suicide due to mental illness.

The Nine of Swords is always a negative card. It is mental and emotional trauma at its most unbearable. Show great care when dealing with the inquirer and always understand your own limitations. Are you *really* qualified to deal with the Nine of Swords?

TEN OF SWORDS
Positive Aspects
- ~ None.

Negative Aspects
- ~ An indication of sudden misfortune including, accidents, assaults or life changing trauma.
- ~ It mental terms, it can be a major blow to ambitions or to the ego, bringing ruin and psychological collapse.

The Ten of Swords is a very negative card - unless it is acting as a warning. But should you really give a warning of assault or danger to the inquirer? Would the warning itself cause even more problems?

PAGE OF SWORDS
Positive Aspects
- ~ As a person, he can be as sharp as steel but can also be a negotiator. He never forgets a fact. He can be very humorous and have a very sharp wit. He may be an amazing talker or linguist.

Negative Aspects
- ~ He may be a bit two-faced or devious. The blade can have two edges! He may also be selfish and too self aware. If representing a child, it can indicate a kind of child progeny who has arrogance and vanity but no great life skills.

KNIGHT OF SWORDS
Positive Aspects
- ~ As a person, the knight can be skillful intellectual and forceful. Always mentally agile and sometimes opinionated. He will have razor sharp intellect and be very fact driven.

Negative Aspects
- ~ The knight can be domineering and pig-headed, but generally challenging and stimulating. May be an unemotional partner who is too cerebral.

QUEEN OF SWORDS

Positive Aspects

~ Normally, she is very perceptive and strong. As can be seen below, she may have had to endure a lot and is justified in feeling sad. She has lightening thoughts and can be wonderful with words or language.

Negative Aspects

~ The card of widowhood. This queen is known as the 'Queen of Sorrows'. She can represent a domineering and intolerant manipulator. She is always quick witted but she is inclined to be a 'nippy sweetie'.

KING OF SWORDS

Positive Aspects

~ This king is intellectual, sharp and decisive. He can be a strong authority figure and can live with a definite moral code. He can also be a great advice giver and have true insight

Negative Aspects

~ This king can be calculating, cold and withdrawn. His ideas may be ones that are firmly bogged down in the past. He may also be scathing and very lacking in social graces.

Homework

Cards

Nine of Swords — King of Swords (6 cards)

Exercise 1

For each of the above 6 cards, thoroughly inspect it, then really look at it for 2-3 minutes and answer the following questions:

(a) Does the card feel positive or negative? (Ignore court cards)

(b) Write down 6 adjectives that you feel best describes the card.

(c)   List the positive and negative aspects of each card.

Exercise 2
Answer the following question using a 21 card spread.

A young mother needs a problem solving reading for her young son. She is so worried for his future. He was born deaf and the first 4 years of his life have been difficult for both of them. She wants to know if he will have a normal and happy life.

The Celtic Cross Spread
This is one of the most difficult spreads to interpret but one that provides a great deal of information, if read correctly. You will find that the positioning of the cards can be flexible. Indeed, American and British interpretations can be quite different and, potentially, confusing.

Try the various forms if you wish, but then decide on one set-up and stick with it. You will be able to become thoroughly familiar with it and enjoy it more.

The Celtic Cross can be used as both a general spread or, as an answering spread for a particular question.

The "significator" card is a card that represents the inquirer.. The significator is normally chosen from the court cards and you can find many interpretations of which to use, including hair and eye colors. My preferences are more basic and I use the following definitions:

Pages - Young people or children.

Knights - Male or female in their 20's and 30's.

Queens - Mature, or married, women.

Kings - Mature, or married, men.

Additionally, the inquirer's astrological sign may be used, i.e.:

Pentacles - Earth signs (Taurus, Virgo & Capricorn)
Cups - Water signs (Cancer, Scorpio & Pisces).
Wands - Fire signs (Aries, Leo & Sagittarius).
Swords - Air signs (Gemini, Libra & Aquarius)

Therefore, a young man whose Sun sign is Cancer would be represented by the Page of Cups; while an Aquarian married woman would be the Queen of Swords.

The Celtic Cross Spread

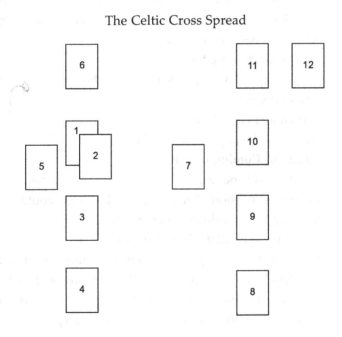

1 Significator
2 Covering   (i.e. Nature of the Problem)
3 Crossing   (i.e. Obstacle or Opposing Force)
4 Below   (i.e. Inner Resources)
5 Behind   (i.e. Waning Energy)
6 Crown   (i.e. Inspiration)
7 Before   (i.e. Coming Influence)
8 Home   (i.e. Immediate Environment)
9 Other People
10 Hopes and Fears
11 Outcome of this Phase
12 Lesson from this Cycle

1. **Significator**

   As above.

2. **Covering or Nature of the Problem**

   What is the problem in the inquirer's life? Are they having difficulties with relationship, career, finances, etc.?

3. **Crossing or Obstacle or Opposing Forces**

   What is the main obstacle to a satisfactory conclusion? What stands in the way of the inquirer?

4. **Below or Inner Resources**

   What aspects of the inquirer's personality can be called on in this situation? What are their strengths? Where do their energies lie? Everyone has inner resources; some people just need them pointed out!

5. **Behind or Waning Energy**

   What happened in the lead up to the problem? What influences are behind it?

6. **Crown or Inspiration**

   How will the inquirer deal with the problem?

7. **Before or Coming Influence**

   What could be around the corner to influence the inquirer's decision? The aspects still to come could affect the inquirer's thinking: what are they?

8. **Home or Immediate Environment**

   What is happening in the environment around the problem? What influences, whether at home or elsewhere, are affecting the decisions to be made? How does the inquirer view themselves within their own space?

9. **Other People**

   Are there people the inquirer can rely on? Could someone else help, or hinder, the outcome? How do others influence the inquirer's state of mind?

10. **Hopes and Fears**

    What are the inquirer's hopes for the future? What are their current, or future, fears? Are the inquirer's hopes sensible, their fears groundless?

11. **Outcome of this Phase**

    What outcome can the inquirer expect? Is it positive or negative? Will it be acceptable to them?

12. **Lesson from this Cycle**

    What can be learned from this cycle of events? Can the inquirer use the situation to grow and develop? Can the lessons learned affect their thought processes or desires?

Homework: Celtic Cross Spread

Exercise 1

Helen is a 40 year old Taurean, going through a difficult relationship with her 16 year old daughter, Emma. Emma is a bright, attractive, talented Gemini who refuses to work at school or in the house. Some of Emma's friends have stolen things from Helen.

Helen had problems of her own in the past, having been sexually abused in her youth with a resultant sense of disempowerment and difficulties with boundaries. She is starting to address some of these issues in therapy. She is also developing considerable psychic abilities.

Helen has been married to her second husband, David, for the last three years. The marriage is a good one, and David is more tolerant than Helen towards Emma. Helen finds the situation with Emma unbearable, as Emma has not responded to discussions in family conferences, or to repeated warnings. Helen is considering throwing Emma out of the family home without any financial support, and telling her to move in with her friends. Helen feels this drastic measure is the only way Emma will be forced to become more mature.

Based on the Celtic Cross spread, with the following cards what do you advise?

1. Ace of Wands
2. Three of Swords
3. Ace of Pentacles
4. Eight of Wands
5. The Devil
6. The Fool
7. Four of Pentacles
8. Six of Cups
9. High Priestess
10. Two of Wands
11. Four of Swords
12. Eight of Swords

Exercise 2

Using the Celtic Cross Spread, answer the following:

An unusually agitated man sits down and asks about his personal life. He says he wants to know what the future hold for him, romantically. He also indicates that his wife left him six weeks ago. His date of birth is 16/5/56.

His chosen cards are:

1. The Lovers.
2. The Star.
3. Ten of Swords.
4. Temperance.
5. The Devil.
6. Ten of Cups.
7. Eight of Swords.
8. Five of Cups.
9. Ace of Cups.
10. The Sun.
11. Ace of Swords
12. Ten of wands

Numerology

Each number is thought to have an essence or a vibration which imparts certain characteristics. When numerology is studied and applied to the Tarot, a greater understanding of each card can be gained. There is also a greater understanding of the flow and build up of events and emotions as we work through the Minor Arcana cards.

Try to learn the numerology and incorporate it into the general meanings of each card. Use the numerology of the Tarot as a guide, or even as an *aide-mémoire*, but remember to be practical in interpretations and do not just regurgitate the meanings of the numbers.

If a number is into double figures, simply add each digit together until it reduces to a single figure.

e.g. The Moon : Card 18 \ 1 + 8 = 9

THE NUMBER 1
Keywords
~ Birth; Creation

Positive Aspects
~ Inspiration to achieve; new beginnings; the force behind creation; the need for independence and clarity of thought; the will to succeed.

Negative Aspects
~ Selfishness; Excessive force; Willful disregard of others.

A lot of 1's in a reading indicate new beginnings and challenges which inspire achievement.

THE NUMBER 2
Keywords
Balance; Co-operation; Application

Positive Aspects

~ A time of waiting and insight; balancing the pro's and cons; The gathering of knowledge before a time of action; Agreement; The balance between the intellect and the imagination.

Negative Aspects

~ Imbalance; Impatience; Indecision

Many 2's in a reading suggest the need to take stock and to balance daily life and the acquisition of the knowledge required for future success.

THE NUMBER 3
Keywords

~ Expression; Communication; Feeling

Positive Aspects

~ After Number 1 (Birth) and Number 2 (Application), the number 3 brings expressions of desires and feelings. Something is about to be brought into being, something which has been aspired to and planned for. The focus tends to be more emotional than intellectual, e.g. self expression, creativity or fun and friendship.

Negative Aspects

~ Delays to plans; Over-indulgence; Activity suspended for a time.

A preponderance of 3's in a reading implies the fulfillment of plans; Group activities and the involvement of more than one person.

THE NUMBER 4
Keywords

~ Realization; Manifestation

Positive Aspects

~ A time when goals are achieved; Strong foundations have been laid and hard work is paying off; Organization and stability; healing through a period of rest and recuperation; the focus is on structure and practical solutions.

Negative Aspects

~ Practical opposition; Excessive structure or materialism.

Sundry 4's in a reading signifies things coming to fruition though hard work and practical choices.

THE NUMBER 5

Keywords

~ Change; Renewal

Positive Aspects

~ The desire for material and spiritual truth; A time of ups and downs and the desire for an in-depth understanding of life; Curiosity and a thirst for a new way of thinking; Opportunity to advance.

Negative Aspects

~ Failure; Defeat; Inability to comprehend changes.

A dominance of 5's in a reading suggests fluctuations, ebb and flow. The need to balance spiritual and material aspects.

THE NUMBER 6

Keywords

~ Adaptability; Adjustment

Positive Aspects

~ Progresses from the Number 5 by acclimatizing to the fluctuations and reaching equilibrium. It brings harmony and balance; and a sense of responsibility and compassion.

Negative Aspects

~ Lack of concern or compassion; Disharmony.

Many 6's in a reading indicate the ability to overcome difficulties and the capacity to offset ups and downs.

THE NUMBER 7

Keywords

~ Faith; Introspection

Positive Aspects

~ Faith and a belief in mysteries yet to unfold; Solitude, self-contemplation and the need to develop spiritually; Striving for perfection.

Negative Aspects

~ Escapism; Fantasy; Fear of the unknown.

A lot of 7's in a reading implies a period of soul searching and personal development.

THE NUMBER 8

Keywords

~ Power; Fortitude

Positive Aspects

~ Power coming from the inner-self that can be harnessed through the understanding and solitude of the Number 7; Spiritual strengthand the ability to cope with challenges; Accomplishment and success.

Negative Aspects

~ Power struggles; Stress; Abuse of power.

Numerous 8's in a reading suggest a change of mind or status brought about by soul-searching or through self-empowerment.

THE NUMBER 9

Keywords

~ Completion; Culmination

Positive Aspects

~ The cycle is almost complete, yet another may be about to begin; Fulfillment and final understanding, particularly in spiritual matters.

Negative Aspects

~ Loss; having to move on from a cherished belief.

A preponderance of 9's in a reading signifies things being completed or finalized, but with a new cycle beginning.

Homework
Exercise 1
Describe the progression of energies, or vibrations, through the sequence of cards Eight of Cups, Nine of Cups, and Ten of Cups.

Exercise 2
Compare and contrast the following pairs of cards, with the emphasis on their numerology:

(a)   The Empress (card 3)
       The Emperor (card 4)
(b)   Justice (card 11)
       The Tower (card 16)

Ethics, Professionalism and
How to do a Professional Reading

Ethics and professionalism

To be ethical is to follow a course of behavior that is seen to be correct, honorable and upholds the morals or beliefs of the individual or group.

To be a professional indicates that you have a level of competence and ability that marks you out from an amateur or person who treats their skill as more of a hobby. It can also indicate that you take payment for your skill. It means that you value your reputation and also, the art of the tarot itself.

Until now, we have concentrated on the meanings of the cards and the interpretation of various spreads using imaginary scenarios. While these can provide good insights, one-to-one, face-to-face readings are very different.

Any potential client who comes to you for a reading is a complex, individual person. They will have many attitudes, beliefs and, possibly, problems that need to be taken into account. They must be dealt with in an ethical way, where personal ethics play a vital role.

While it is essential to interpret the cards accurately you must use careful judgment when deciding whether to tell the inquirer all, or how much of what you see in their cards. A client must never leave a reading with more worries than when they came in!

Carry out all your readings with a high degree of professionalism. Rushing, over-familiarity and slap-dash attitudes are some of the factors which can contribute to an unsatisfactory reading.

If you accept payment for a reading you should be confident in your abilities, as well as being certain of the cards and your techniques. Otherwise, you are simply not ready to charge a fee and you must do more practice spreads.

Unless you have a recognized counseling qualification, remember that you have no right to set yourself up as a counselor. You can only advise the client on what you see in the cards. You can certainly indicate the options that you see are open to them but never, ever tell anyone what to do. Always leave the inquirer to make their own choices.

Be aware that you, and every reader, is fallible and there is a chance that your interpretation may be wrong. Do not be so foolhardy or egotistic not to realize that you have limitations.

Once you have considered what is important to you, you may want to write down your own personal code of ethics (see homework) . When you have done so, try not to make excuses or to deviate from your moral code. You may find some of the following guidelines useful.

Always avoid telling an inquirer what to do. Offer them the options as you see them, but emphasize that the ultimate choice is theirs.

- Never give the impression that you are an expert in any field, such as counseling, financial services, life coaching etc., unless you are actually qualified in it.

- Be wary of answering questions about a third party. It is an entirely different matter to give your opinion on a question about a child's school success than to answer a question like "Is my sister's husband having an affair?"

- Never pass on any personal tragedies, or possible deaths, that you see in the cards. Nobody is 100% accurate 100% of the time and you could cause untold damage and mental anguish.

- Do not read for someone that you consider mentally

unstable or traumatized. They will not be in the right frame of mind for a reading and may take the wrong meaning from it. They need help from a health professional, not you.

- Avoid making the client feel nervous or intimidated. Try to distance yourself from the clichéd image of the funfair fortune-teller with spooky paraphernalia. You are a professional person. All you require is your intuition, knowledge and your Tarot deck. However, if you follow a particular path and it is truly part of you, connections to it e.g. Wicca/Christian/shamanic jewelry, would be acceptable if not overdone. Think about *who* you are and if an embellishment is not part of your personality and is simply for show...take it off!

- Never let your own personal belief system, religion or outlook interfere with giving good advice. Never judge a persons actions e.g. on an abortion, an affair or an addiction. There for the grace of god etc!

Tarot Readings

Provided you have the knowledge, the skills, the experience and your personal code of ethics you should be ready to give a really professional reading. The following points may help you read in a more relaxed and enjoyable style.

I have also included warnings and suggestions of acceptable standards. I do not mean to offend in any way but I have, unfortunately, seen certain practices and attitudes that tend to bring the profession into disrepute. I want to help you avoid these pitfalls.

Setting Up

- Make sure that you have a comfortable chair, and a table

that is both large enough, and also the correct height with which to work.

- Try to get yourself as comfortable as possible, even if you are in unfamiliar surroundings.

- Designate your own space and place your cards, tape recorder, etc. in positions that you feel are attractive and appealing. Consider carrying your own tablecloth.

- Avoid using tatty or grubby old cards. The tarot is beautiful to behold and should be a pleasure to handle and view. Using a dirty deck shows disrespect for your inquirer. Of course, if you have a very favorite deck that has been discontinued, you may have cards that are past their best. Then, this becomes a very personal decision. In recent years, I have provided antiseptic hand gel for clients who wished it and have used this gel in between readings myself. This seems to have helped guard me against flu bugs. (It can also help prevent infection of the tiny paper cuts that can be a side affect of using a new deck!)

- Take about 30 minutes to relax and tune in to the energies around you. Ensure you can switch off from all the background noises around you. It is very rare to consult in total silence. Meditate using your favorite crystals, prayers or mantra. Allow your third eye to open.

The Reading

- Welcome the inquirer in a friendly, professional manner. Do not be over-familiar or condescending. Try to just be natural. Ask their name and note it down so you will not forget it or call them by the wrong name. Make a note of their date of birth or star sign. This will help you identify them in the spread.

- Follow an established pattern that you feel comfortable with, e.g. familiar spreads, familiar cards and opening and closing words or phrases.

- Speak clearly at all times. Do not mumble or speak too softly. Avoid slang and, obviously, swearing is totally out of order! Avoid covering your mouth with hands or gestures or you will make the reading difficult for hearing impaired people.

- Do not rush. If you need to contemplate the cards in silence for a few seconds, do not worry. Explain this to the inquirer, if you feel it necessary. Think carefully, and do not just blurt out your first impressions. As you become more proficient the number and length of pauses will decrease.
- Set a standard time for a reading and try not to overrun. You do yourself no favors by extending a reading as:

  1. You will tire more quickly.

  2. Other clients may be irate at having to wait.

I normally have a clock behind the inquirer that I can glance at - without being too obvious!

- Thank the client for coming to see you. Add that they should not come back before a specified period of time has elapsed. Discourage them if they try to return too soon. Some people will use readings as a crutch which can then become an addiction.

- If you charge a fee, take it at the end of the reading. This allows you judge if you have been worth it. Never take money if you think you have been below par or have simply not received anything from your cards. Do not read for people if you are ill or have an infectious cough or cold.

- Relax for 5 - 10 minutes between clients. Never appear to be hurried or rushed. Avoid giving any indications that you may be having a hard day or are feeling stressed. This is not about you!

Further Points

- Present yourself well. Take care of your appearance. Hands will be a focus! Dress well and avoid clichéd clothes: a business suit may be more appropriate than looking like you escaped from Hogwarts!

- Give yourself an air of confidence. If you cannot believe in yourself, why should your client?

- Never belittle another reader or practitioner, even if the inquirer wants to gossip/complain about them.

- Before the reading begins make sure the inquirer understands the charges and the length of the reading. It is also important to state any legality which is necessary e.g. *'all readings are for entertainment purposes only, have not been scientifically proven and are for over 18's only. This reading is not a substitute for professional advice from e.g. a doctor, financial advisor or other relevant professional'*. I carry a typed sign to place on my table and also read it to clients. You may feel 'cheapened' or annoyed at having to say this, but if it is the law, then it has to be done. Always say that the cards 'suggest' a course of action or 'suggest' an outcome. Never tell a client what to do. I believe that the cards always provide the answers, but your interpretation could be wrong or not as accurate as it could be. Don't be arrogant! You are not above being wrong or the laws of the country.

- Take time to find out what is legal in your country or state and make sure you carry personal indemnity insurance if it is a legal requirement. This is your responsibility and because of different legal systems, cannot be covered here. Don't take risks!

- Try to enjoy yourself!!

Homework
Exercise 1
Write down the names of 6 people who you feel epitomize the word "professional". What is special about them? How do they inspire you? What are their main characteristics? See if there are any themes or similarities in this list and let it show you what you can aspire to and what is really important to you.

Exercise 2
Produce your own personal code of ethics.

Analyze your own morality. Think how you would like to be treated. Explain why you have reached those conclusions that differ from, or are additional to, the guidelines given.

Exercise 3
Find out the legal requirements of your country or state and make a notice out of card for your reading table. Look into any indemnity insurances you may need.

And finally...if you have followed this book, learned the cards and spreads and decided on your professional and ethical codes, then you are equipped with the information to start doing readings for others. But you will need to practice, practice and then practice more. Every time you do a reading, you will learn more about the card meanings and your own ability. Remember each reading, take notes and go back over your insights or worries. Write a journal of your feelings, any problems that presented ethically and how you handled them. And practice some more.

You may then want to delve deeper into the cards and have a more in depth understanding of them. You may decide to find out more about the astrological aspects of the cards, or the meaning of certain symbols or letters on the original decks. You may be interested in a deck that corresponds with your own spirituality e.g. shaman, Wicca, and pursue a greater under-standing of this. Let yourself be guided and go at your own pace. And practice some more!

One of the greatest compliments I have received was when someone said that 'I saw all life situations as tarot cards' and I do! In the tarot, real life is represented in each card, different card combinations and in the way it flows. By practicing and adding to your understanding, you will begin to 'live' the tarot. In my opinion, it's a good way to live!

DODONA
BOOKS

Dodona Books offers a broad spectrum of divination systems to
suit all, including Astrology, Tarot, Runes, Ogham, Palmistry,
Dream Interpretation, Scrying, Dowsing, I Ching, Numerology,
Angels and Faeries, Tasseomancy and Introspection.

9781846949654